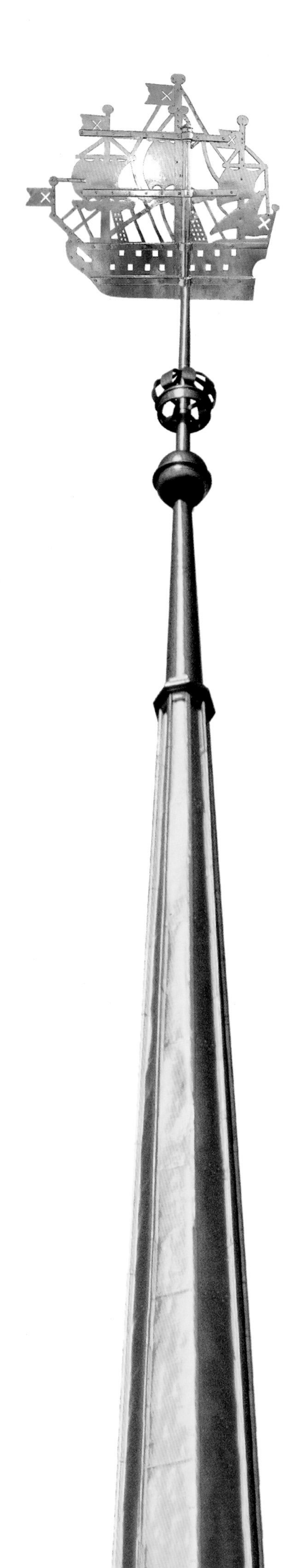

# SAINT PETERSBURG

ИВАН ФЕДОРОВ

*I love thee, Peter's bold creation,*
*I love thy air austere, thy lone*
*Great squares, and Neva's fascination*
*Between her banks of granite stone...*

*Alexander Pushkin*

# SAINT PETERSBURG

## PETERHOF
## TSARSKOYE SELO
## PAVLOVSK
## GATCHINA
## ORANIENBAUM
## KRONSTADT

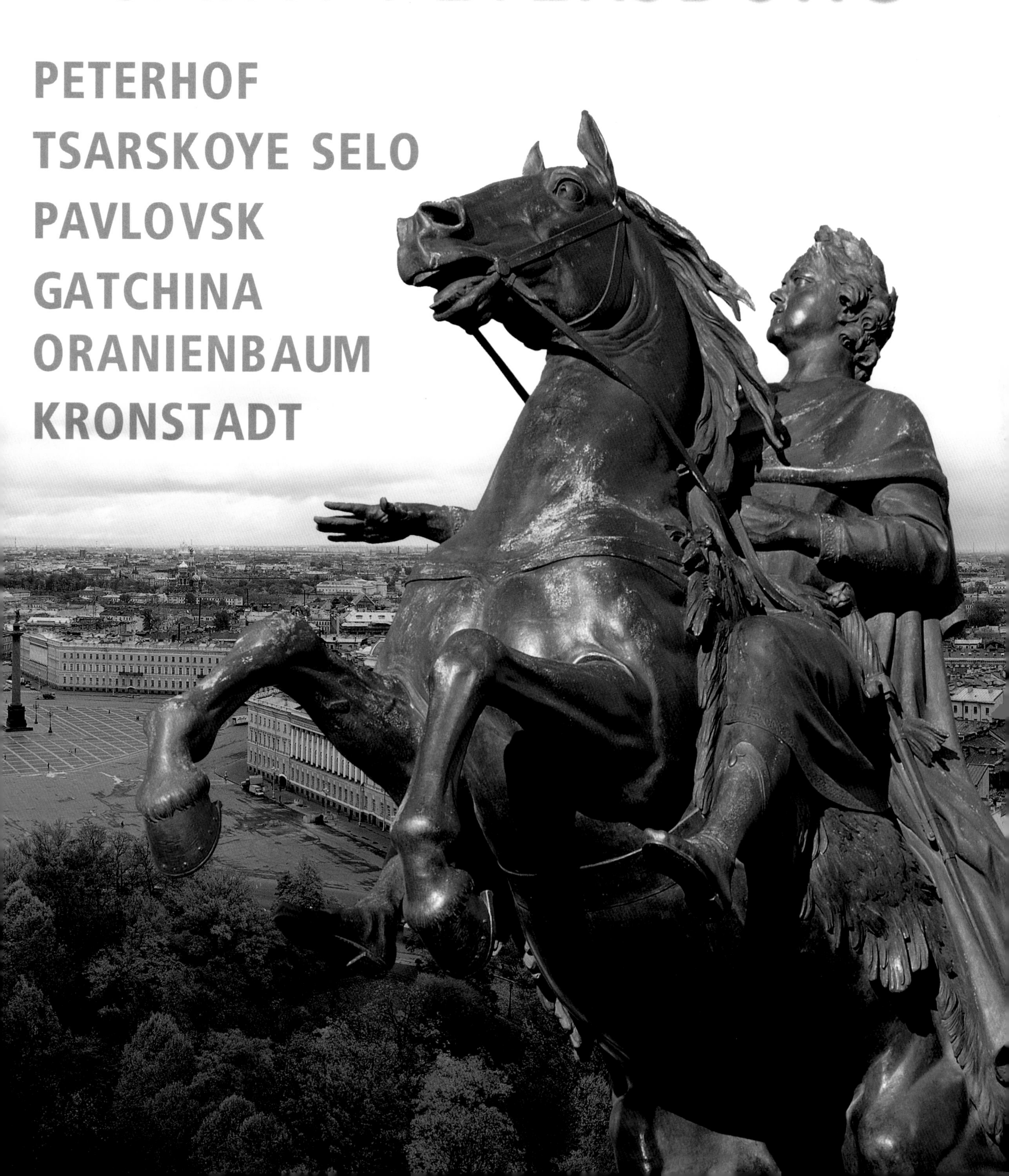

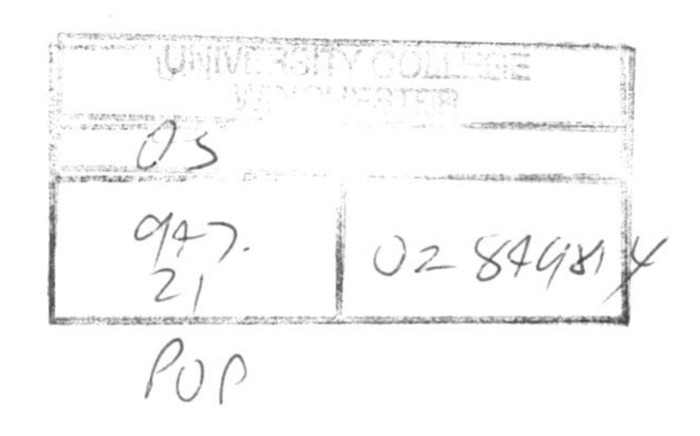


Text

Natalia Popova and Andrei Fedorov

Translation

Gillian Kenyon

Design

Nikolai Kutovoy and Evgueny Kutovoy

Photographs

Serguei Alexeev, Vladimir Antoshchenkov, Valentin Baranovsky, Nikolai Berketov, Leonid Bogdanov, Sergei Chistobaev, Vladimir Davydov, Pavel Demidov, Vladimir Denisov, Vladimir Filippov, Alexander Fomichev, Leonid Gerkus, Eduard Gorbatenko, Alexander Gronsky, Alexander Kashnitsky, Leonard Kheifets, Artur Kirakozov, Pavel Kuzmichev, Mikhail Manin, Vladimir Melnikov, Yury Molodkovets, Nikolai Rakhmanov, Alexander Riazantsev, Viktor Savik, Georgy Shablovsky, Nikolai Shalyakin, Vladimir Shlakan, Evgueny Shlepkin, Evgueny Siniaver, Vladimir Terebenin, Oleg Trubsky, Vasily Vorontsov, Leonid Yakutin, Kira Zharinova

Editors

Irina Kharitonova, Irina Lvova

English text editor

Elena Shabalova

Computer layout

Elena Morozova

Colour correction

Viacheslav Bykovski, Ekaterina Fomenko, Vladimir Glaskov, Vladimir Kniazev, Alexander Kondratov, Liubov Kornilova, Denis Lazarev, Serguei Ludzski, Alexander Miagkov, Dmitry Trofimov, Serguei Vyrtosu



ISBN 5-93893-090-1

Printed and bound in Russia

The city of St Petersburg, the former capital of the Russian Empire and the embodiment of the pride and glory of the Russian state, was founded on 27 May 1703. The creation of the city was a daring feat. In order to realise his vision, Peter I, turning his back on the traditions of "ancient" Rus, called upon the new generation, which, with its fierce confidence and characteristic youthfulness, welcomed his ambitious plans. St Petersburg became the symbol of a new era of Russian history and grandiose, unprecedented ventures. As if challenging nature itself, the Emperor resolved to create a northern "Paradise" on an area of marshy land that seemed perpetually wreathed in mist. Petersburg became the primary concern and favourite "child of the northern giant, in which the energy, brutality and revolutionary force of the '93 Convention were concentrated, ... [the favourite child] of the tsar, who renounced his country for its own good and oppressed it in the name of Europeanism and civilisation" (Alexander Herzen). Indeed, the building of the new capital demanded a concerted effort and a great deal of strength. Many thousands of human lives were lost in the process, and it is perhaps because of this that the history of Petersburg is so full of dark and tragic events. During the three hundred years of its existence, it has endured more than its fair share of historical and natural disasters.

In times of war, hostile forces have tried again and again to capture the city, thinking to erase it from the face of the earth, but not once has an army succeeded in setting foot within its limits. Even the most terrifying blockade in the history of mankind, lasting 872 days from 8 September 1941 to 27 January 1944, was unable to break the spirit of the city's inhabitants.

In the autumn, the merciless elements threaten to wreak havoc on the long, flat banks of the River Neva. Three terrible deluges, which have occurred with an alarming regularity every hundred years (1724, 1824 and 1924), and other less significant floods have sought to destroy this man-made wonder, yet the city has stood its ground.

The unpredictability of the elements makes Petersburg a profoundly expressive city. It has the ability to change its countenance unexpectedly, compelling us to see its beauty in a new light. It is as if the city senses the mood of its inhabitants and seeks to share with them both their joy and melancholy. The most enchanting time, however, is that of the famous White Nights, which last from mid-May to mid-July, when the city casts its spell over locals and visitors alike. These few months seem almost to compensate for the frequent rains, clammy mists, short winter days and long autumn nights. "A multitude of poets have extolled and described our northern nights, but to express their beauty in words is as impossible as describing the scent of a rose and the tremor of a string fading into air. No poet can convey the inexpressible, mysterious silence, pregnant with thoughts and life, that rests on the heavily respiring Neva after the heat of day in the phospho-

rescent light of the frail clouds and crimson west. No painter can capture the wondrous shades and hues that play in the sky and are reflected in the rivers as on the skin of a chameleon, in the facets of crystal or the polarisation of light. No musician can transpose into earthly tongues the sounds, permeated with feeling, that rise up from the earth to the skies only to fall back to earth once more reflected by the heavens" (Apollon Grigoriev).

St Petersburg is the "strangest of all Russian cities." It is a unique entity with a highly pronounced individuality and a complex and subtle spirit, which leads a mysterious, dramatic life of its own. No other Russian city is the subject of so many myths and legends. No other city has aroused such mixed responses from the very moment it was born: it has been loved and hated, lauded and damned, but it has left no one indifferent. "What a city! What a river! An unparalleled city! One must part with Petersburg for a short time and see the old capitals, ramshackle Paris and sooty London, in order to appreciate Petersburg's worth. Look what harmony! How all the parts complement the whole! Such beautiful buildings, such taste and altogether such variety springing from the union of water and buildings." Dating from the early 19th century, these are the words of the famous Russian poet Konstantin Batiushkov, a man with a keen sense of the beauty of Petersburg.

The reason why this most "contrived" city is so remarkable is that "its appearance bears the mark of a deliberate human creation." It began with thoughts and ideas laid out in a plan.

The open stretches of dry land and the lines of the Neva and the canals became formative elements in the design of Petersburg. Here, emphasis was placed less on erecting individual buildings than on creating entire artificial panoramas. Architects were careful to contrive long vistas. The idiosyncrasies of the design of the northern capital can be seen clearly from a bird's eye view. "Everything appears flat, the city's unevenness is erased, and before us lies a faintly outlined relief, like a plan. Yet the observer is able to see the city within the framework of nature. It is as if nature is closing in on the city, while the city casts its reflection on the surrounding landscape" (Nikolai Antsiferov).

Petersburg also owes its uniqueness to its geographical location: it stands on the edge of the vast territory of Russia and is indeed a "window onto Europe". From the west it has not only been buffeted by the waters of the autumn floods, but also by the shocks of historic disasters endured by the West. European ideas and the joys and woes of the "old continent" have been borne in on the Baltic winds.

St Petersburg threw its doors open wide to everyone who accepted the invitation to take part in the ambitious and rather risky business of its creation. The young city was notable for its receptivity to the cultural achievements of Europe and the knowledge and skills of its foreign guests. In other countries, schools were established first, followed by universities, and only once a significant number of scholars had emerged were academies founded. In Peter's day, the first schools were only beginning to take shape in Russia and not a single university existed, yet the tsar-reformer

had already decided to invite learned foreigners (mainly from Germany) to Petersburg to create an Academy of Sciences. He offered them the opportunity to conduct scientific research at the expense of the state in return for introducing young Russian men to the principles of science.

Artists, architects, sculptors and engravers were also invited to Russia to sow the seeds of the European fine arts in the damp soil on the banks of the Neva. Petersburg swiftly absorbed and assimilated all things beautiful. Germans, Swedes, Italians, Dutch-, French- and Englishmen initially made their homes in separate colonies, but the national and linguistic boundaries gradually disappeared. Within a short time, a unique nation had arisen – the nation of Petersburg, in which locals and Russified foreigners lived in harmony.

For many who came to Petersburg, the city became a second home to which they devoted their energy and talents. Together with Russian experts, they worked to create a city and build splendid country residences for the ruling elite. Some people believe that "Petersburg doesn't have an ounce of originality: it is simply a kind of general embodiment of the notion of a capital city, and is the spit and image of any other major city in the world" (Vissarion Belinsky). Yet nothing could be further from the truth. European architectural forms metamorphosed under the influences of Russian architecture, resulting in the emergence of genuinely unique edifices. In art, as in the social and everyday life of the city, European and Russian traditions merged to create an entirely new phenomenon – the culture of St Petersburg.

### The Peter and Paul Fortress

For the first few years, construction work was centred on Hare Island. Here, the fortress of Sankt Pieter Burkh was erected as the nucleus of the future city. Its location was selected by Peter the Great himself who well understood the strategic advantages of placing such an outpost on the island in the Neva delta. Within a year, six bastions (the projecting portions of a fortification) had been raised. Although the bastions were made of earth (substituted with stone in 1740), building the new city out of stone was one of Peter's greatest concerns. A special decree was issued prohibiting the construction of stone edifices elsewhere in Russia, and all master stonemasons were ordered to the banks of the Neva. Peter also introduced an unusual "stone toll": every boat and every string of carts to enter the city had to bring a certain number of stones with it.
The fortress was designed as a closed rampart consisting of bastions and curtains (the part of the wall connecting the bastions). Peter was in a hurry to complete the job before the winter and so the construction of the fortifications was carried out under the supervision of the tsar's closest associates, thus the bastions are named in honour of these men, to wit, Naryshkin, Trubetskoy, Zotov, Golovkin and Menshikov. One of the southern bastions was built under the direct observation of Peter himself and consequently became known as the Tsar Bastion.
On the eastern side of the island, in the curtain that links the Tsar Bastion with the Menshikov Bastion, the main gates to the fortress – St Peter's Gate – were installed. They were protected by a ravelin (a V-shaped outwork incorporated into the design of the ramparts), which was named in honour of Saint John. In order to get into the fortress it was necessary to cross the wooden St John's Bridge, pass through St John's Gate and then through a second gateway – St Peter's Gate (built in stone to replace the original wooden structure in1714–1718, architect: Domenico Trezzini). The triumphal arch of the latter still bears a beautifully preserved double-headed eagle (the coat-of-arms of the Russian Empire) wearing imperial crowns, made of lead and weighing over a tonne.
Beyond St Peter's Gate the path is lined by two squat military buildings: to the right is the Artillery Arsenal (1801), and to the left is the Engineer's House (1749).
By 1787, the entire fortress was clad in granite. A signal tower and flagpole for a special fortress standard, were installed on the Naryshkin Bastion, which also became the site of a cannon, fired every day at noon, a tradition that has been preserved to this day.
The main building within the fortress is the Sts Peter and Paul Cathedral.

Its shape is somewhat reminiscent of that of an 18th century ship: the high eastern wall is the stern, while the tall spire is the mast. This belfry together with the gilded spire and figure of an angel, the guardian of the city, stands at a height of 122.5 metres. At the time it was the tallest building in Russia. The figure of the angel serves as a weather vane, indicating the direction of the wind. Stretching boldly towards the heavens, the cathedral spire became an integral part of the Petersburg skyline from the moment it first appeared.

Not far from the Sts Peter and Paul Cathedral is the Commandant's House (1743–1746) in which the commanding officer of the fortress lived. Over the course of two hundred years there were 32 commandants. It was an honoured position and was often held for life. It was awarded to generals of great merit who had earned the particular trust of the sovereign.

In 1992, a statue of Peter I, the work of Mikhail Shemiakin, was erected on the square in front of the guardhouse and soon became the subject of great debate. This unusual image is quite different to the typical representations of the tsar-creator and tsar-victor that prevailed in the monumental sculptures of centuries gone by. Yet the longer the statue "lives" in the fortress, the more normal its presence becomes. Peter calmly observes the inquisitive tourists, poses for their cameras and pays no attention to the children who today know no fear of the "bronze shadow" of the formidable Emperor.

**1**
White Nights. Peter and Paul Fortress seen from the Trinity Bridge

**2**
Entrance to the Peter and Paul Fortress

**3**
View from the belfry of the Sts Peter and Paul Cathedral

**4**
View of St John's Gate

**5**
St Peter's Gate. 1714–1718, architect: Domenico Trezzini
sculptors: Hans Konrad Osner, Nicolas Pinod

## The Sts Peter and Paul Cathedral

The design of the church, including the decorative fittings inside, is indicative of the typical Petersburg practice of combining the traditions of western religious architecture and Ancient Russian church design. Thus, the interior of the cathedral includes both a carved wooden iconostasis executed after the Orthodox traditions, and a carved pulpit for the preacher, as in a Catholic church.
The interior of the cathedral is designed like a ceremonial hall, divided by piers into three naves. Its main feature is the carved gilded iconostasis (1722–1729, designed by the architects Domenico Trezzini and Ivan Zarudny). The central section of the iconostasis resembles a triumphal arch, a symbolic celebration of the glorious victory of the Russian troops in the Northern War. The lavishness and grandeur of the architectural forms of this altar screen combined with countless sculptures creates the kind of stunning decorative effect that is typical of the Baroque style. Beyond the *tsarskie vrata* (*the royal gates* or central doors in the iconostasis) there is a richly decorated canopy over the table used in the performance

**6**
Domes and belfry of the Sts Peter and Paul Cathedral
**7**
Peter and Paul Fortress. View of Cathedral Square
Sts Peter and Paul Cathedral.
1712–1733, architect: Domenico Trezzini.
Boat House. 1762–1765, architect: Alexander Vist
**8**
Commandant's House. Memorial Hall
**9**
Statue of Peter I. 1992, sculptor: Mikhail Shemiakin

of religious ceremonies. It was fashioned after Lorenzo Bernini's canopy in St Peter's Cathedral in Rome.

In the 1830s, in the right-hand row of piers, the *imperial (tsar's) place* was installed, made up of a small dais under a carved wooden canopy where the Emperor or Empress would stand during services. The canopy is decorated with drapes of raspberry velvet and its carved peak is crowned with the representation of a pillow bearing the royal regalia. Opposite the *tsar's place* is the pulpit, decorated with wooden statues of the Apostles Peter and Paul, the four Evangelists and the Holy Spirit in the form of a dove surrounded by clouds and cherubim. The pulpit is additionally decorated with paintings on Gospel subjects. This splendid example of Russian woodcarving was installed here in 1732. The Sts Peter and Paul Cathedral contains a significant collection of paintings from the Petrine era. The face of the iconostasis incorporates 43 icons, set out somewhat differently to those in the Russian Orthodox churches. The royal gates themselves are unusual – four panels covered with depictions of the Last Supper in bas-relief, and not a single icon in sight.

**10**
Sts Peter and Paul Cathedral. The tsar's place and the pulpit

**11**
Sts Peter and Paul Cathedral. The tsar's place. Detail

**12**
Sts Peter and Paul Cathedral. Interior

**13**
Sts Peter and Paul Cathedral. Iconostasis
1722–1729, designed by Ivan Zarudny

**14–16**
Sts Peter and Paul Cathedral. Iconostasis
Icons: *Queen Bathsheba, Holy Prince Vladimir, Holy Prince Alexander Nevsky*
Mid-18th century, artists: Alexei Protopopov, Andrei Pospelov

ЦРЦА ВЕРСАВИА

КНЗЬ · ВЛАДИМІРЪ

КНЗЬ
АЛЕЗАНДРЪ НЕВСКИ

**The Peter and Paul Fortress – a witness to Russian history**

The Peter and Paul Fortress never served a direct military purpose, since no enemy ever made it as far as its walls. Very soon after it had been built, however, it began to be used as a political prison and torture-chamber. Over the course of two hundred years, its bastions and casemates held countless enemies of the state.
To the southwest of the cathedral a ravelin was constructed, which was later named in honour of Tsarevich Alexei. It is to this place above all that the infamy of the Peter and Paul Fortress is linked. In February 1718, Peter I brought his own son, Alexei, here together with a number of other conspirators. After enduring horrific tortures, conducted, so historians claim, in the presence of the Emperor himself, Alexei was executed. Throughout the 18th century, many people experienced the horrors of the fortress's casemates. In the 19th century, the chambers in the bastions and the Secret House of the Alexeevsky Ravelin built in the reign of Paul I were never empty. In April 1849, for example, a large number of men who had been arrested in connection with the case of Butashevich-Petrashevsky were brought here, including the twenty-eight year old Dostoevsky.
In one of the rooms of the Commandant's House, now the Memorial Hall, the Supreme Criminal Court would convene to hear the cases of the many political prisoners held in the Peter and Paul Fortress. Thus, on 12 July 1826, five Decembrists – Ryleev, Pestel, Muraviev-Apostol, Bestuzhev-Riumin and Kakhovsky – were sentenced to death. These men had been responsible for the first protest for freedom, the Constitution and human rights in Russia. One of the many places of incarceration that existed at different times within the fortress was the prison in the Trubetskoy Bastion (1708–1714). Those who died in solitary confinement within its walls, plagued by the stench and the damp, heard the melodious chimes of the Sts Peter and Paul Cathedral before they died. The last prisoners to be held in the Trubetskoy Bastion, from 1917–1919, were the ministers of the Provisional Government and the Grand Dukes.
The cathedral is the imperial burial-vault. The tomb of Peter the Great is marked with the standards of the regiments which, under his leadership, conquered the Swedes in the Northern War (1700–1721). All of the Emperors and Grand Dukes lie under identical white marble sarcophagi, save for Alexander II and his wife Maria Alexandrovna, who was born a princess of Hessen-Darmstadt. Their graves are marked by sarcophagi made of coloured jasper by the workers of the Urals' plants as a sign of their gratitude for the abolition of serfdom. In 1998, the remains of the last Russian Emperor, Nicholas II, and the various members of his family who were shot to death in Ekaterinburg in June 1918, were buried in the cathedral.

**17**
Emperor Nicholas II. Photograph

**18**
Empress Alexandra Fedorovna. Photograph

**19**
Sts Peter and Paul Cathedral
Tombs of Peter the Great, Catherine I and Elizabeth Petrovna. 1865, architect: Auguste Poirot

**20**
Sts Peter and Paul Cathedral.
St Catherine Side-chapel. Grave of the last Emperor, Nicholas II, his wife, Alexandra Fedorovna, their children and members of the household

**21**
Peter and Paul Fortress. Catherine Curtain.
1710–1727, architect: Domenico Trezzini.
Neva Gate. 1784–1787, architect: Nikolai Lvov

## Vasilievsky Island

After it had been decreed in 1712 that the imperial court was to move from Moscow to the banks of the Neva, the northern city began to be developed in accordance with a plan that had been drawn up previously by local and foreign experts. Vasilievsky Island was originally intended to become the heart of the emerging city. Peter was particularly fond of Amsterdam and hoped that the new capital would somehow remind him of that place. It was planned to create a network of streets and canals, which would drain the marshy land, on Vasilievsky Island. Although this project was not brought to completion, the right-angled arrangement of the streets and the three main avenues which form the architectural basis of the area today almost coincides with the initial plan. The so-called Bolshoy (Large), Sredny (Medium), and Maly (Small) Prospekts run from west to east and are intersected from north to south by 34 "lines", which open out onto the Neva.

For a hundred years this was the site of the city's port. At the beginning of the 19th century, it was moved further downstream, and now only the wrought iron rings set in the granite walls of the embankment serve as a reminder of the fact that ships once moored here. The spit of Vasilievsky Island was designed to reflect Petersburg's status as an international centre of shipping and commerce. The centrepiece of the resulting architectural composition is the Stock Exchange, which resembles a Doric-style temple, hence its nickname the "Russian Parthenon". The main façade, overlooking the Neva, is adorned with the figures of the sea god Neptune and his retinue, while on the western side an allegorical embodiment of Navigation stands alongside the god of commerce, Mercury. Although Mercury is no longer worshipped here, the building remains faithful to the fierce god of the sea: today, the Stock Exchange is the home of the Naval Museum.

**22**
Panoramic view of the Neva and Vasilievsky Island

From 1724 to 1734, the building known as the Twelve Collegia was constructed on Vasilievsky Island. The first major administrative establishment in the city, it was intended to house the twelve different government departments, a fact that was reflected in its unique architectural design. Since 1819, it has been occupied by the University of Petersburg.
The first building to be constructed facing the Neva during the Petrine era was the *Kunstkammer*, which became the city's first public museum.

**23**
Stock Exchange (Naval Museum). 1805–1816, architect: Jean-François Thomas de Thomon

**24**
Naval Museum display inside the Stock Exchange

**25**
View of the University Embankment. Academy of Sciences. 1783–1789, architect: Giacomo Quarenghi
*Kunstkammer*. 1718–1734, architects: Georg Mattarnovi, Gaetano Chiaveri and Mikhail Zemtsov

**26**
Institute of Russian Literature ("Pushkin House"). 1829–1832, architect: Giovanni Luchini

**27**
Rostral Column. 1805–1810,
sculptors: Georges Camberlain, François Thibault.
1810, architect: Jean-François Thomas de Thomon

## The Menshikov Palace

In the early 18th century, the city's first and largest estate, the property of Peter I's close associate and the first governor of Petersburg, Alexander Menshikov, was built. Today, only the palace remains, overlooking the Neva and equipped with its own pier. The only one of its kind in Petersburg at the time, the palace was used to receive ambassadors and host the Petersburg "assemblies" at which Peter the Great taught European etiquette to the boyars who had moved north from Moscow. The palace grew together with the city, in the 1710s it stood out with its three large storeys, tall copper clad mansard roof and wide portico supporting a balcony from which guests approaching by river were greeted by music in the Venetian manner. Menshikov's life ended in tragedy. In 1727, two years after the death of the first Russian Emperor, he was stripped of his rank and wealth and banished from Petersburg with his family. Menshikov soon died in exile. His palace was confiscated and turned over to the state. From the 1730s, the main building, together with new premises built on Menshikov's vast estate, housed the cadet corps. The palace has survived to this day with very few changes and is now a valuable monument to the architecture of the first third of the 18th century.

**28**
Menshikov Palace. 1710s–1720s, architects:
Giovanni Mario Fontana, Gottfried Johann Schaedel

**29**
Unknown 18th-century artist
*Portrait of Alexander Menshikov*

**30**
Menshikov Palace. Grand Hall

## The Academy of Arts

The building was erected after the founding of the Academy (1757) on the site of the houses of Petrine dignitaries. For a number of years, classes were actually held in these homes. The Petersburg Academy of Arts was the first educational establishment of its type in Russia. To this day, Russian artists, sculptors and architects are trained there.
In the early 19th century, a flight of granite steps leading down to the water was created in front of the Academy after designs by the architect Konstantin Thon. Since 1834, the stretch of embankment before the majestic bulk of the Academy of Arts has been guarded by a pair of sphinxes with the face of Amenhotep III, who was in power when the kingdom of Egypt was flourishing.

**31**
University Embankment. Pier in front of the Academy of Arts
1832–1834, architect: Konstantin Thon
Sphinx (Egypt, 13th century B.C.)

**32**
Rumiantsev Obelisk in the Rumiantsev Gardens. 1799,
architect: Vincenzo Brenna, sculptor: Pierre-Louis Agie

**33**
Academy of Arts. 1764–1788, architects: Jean-Baptiste Vallin de La Mothe,
Alexander Kokorinov

**34**
Academy of Arts Museum. Copies of antique sculptures

## Vasilievsky Island – the maritime heart of St Petersburg

The abundance of water and the open skies above the flat, cheerless banks of the river, broken by the mouths of countless smaller channels, set the tone for the architectural development of Petersburg and determined its regular layout. Pride of place was given to the main waterway, the Neva.

Downstream from the Lieutenant Schmidt Bridge, freight ships, tankers and tourist liners from far and wide line the banks of Vasilievsky Island and the English Embankment. Occasionally, one of the few large sailboats that are still in use will winter here. Floating restaurants in the guise of old vessels can be seen on the Neva all year round, however. On very rare occasions, when Petersburg happens to be one of the finishing points of the international Cutty Sark Tall Ships' Races, the river becomes crowded with sailboats and the façades of the elegant residences lining the banks are obscured by a forest of masts and rigging.

**35**
Lieutenant Schmidt Bridge and the English Embankment seen from the Lieutenant Schmidt Embankment

**36**
Lieutenant Schmidt Embankment
Statue of Admiral Krusenstern
1873, sculptor: Ivan Schroeder

**37**
View of Palace Bridge raised

**38**
International Cutty Sark Tall Ships' Races on the Neva

**St Andrew's Cathedral and the Mining Institute**

Contrary to Peter's wishes, Vasilievsky Island did not become the centre of Petersburg. The river, wide and restless, particularly in the autumn, became a serious hindrance, hampering the link between the island and the mainland of the northern capital. Nonetheless, the architectural idea that was first conceived and partly realised in the development of this area of Petersburg became the guiding aesthetic principle for the entire city.
The Neva became the main "street", and houses were erected in a single row along its banks, following the line of the river as it snaked along its course. The fundamental principle of orderliness and regularity was likewise applied during the development of the city centre. Moreover, in response to a proposal from Peter himself, the architect Domenico Trezzini developed three types of building for the three main social groups within the population of Petersburg, making the buildings of approximately equal height. The skyline created by these almost uniform structures seemed to mirror the long straight lines of the natural landscape.
The old part of Vasilievsky Island is a unique monument to the 18th century. More than any other region of Petersburg, it reflects the architectural plans of the Petrine era. Not only the public buildings, including houses of worship, but the many residential buildings too have more or less retained their original appearance.
St Andrew's Cathedral, on the corner of Bolshoy Prospekt and the sixth line, is particularly remarkable. This wooden cathedral was the first church in Russia to be dedicated to an order. Following the common practice in all European countries, Peter founded a supreme order of state, known as the Order of St Andrew, the apostle who, as legend has it, brought Christianity to pagan Rus. Apart from the Russian Emperors and their heirs, dignitaries of the highest rank were decorated with this order for acts of great merit. St Andrew's Cathedral was rebuilt in stone after the original building was destroyed by fire in 1761. Inside, a carved wooden iconostasis of great artistic value can be seen to this day.
Classicism, the dominant architectural style of the late 18th – early 19th century, first emerged in Petersburg architecture in the design of the Academy of Arts, which stands at the furthest end of the University Embankment and plays an important role in the architectural ensemble on the banks of the Neva. The principles of Classicism are also

clearly illustrated by the compact and regular edifice of the Academy of Sciences with its austere façade, mighty eight-column portico and double staircase so typical of Petersburg. The panorama of the banks of Vasilievsky Island is completed by the majestic façade of the Mining Institute (1806–1811, architect: Andrei Voronikhin). This edifice was intended to decorate the city's entrance from the sea, and was thus designed to be seen from afar. Its grandiose twelve-column portico against the backdrop of a rusticated wall is indeed extremely striking from the water.
Moreover, the Mining Institute is a monument to Late Classicism, characterised by the synthesis of architecture and sculpture. Two sculptural groups embodying the philosophical notions behind the building adorn the steps that lead up to the colonnade. To the right is "Pluto Carrying Off Proserpina" (1809–1811, sculptor: Vasily Demut-Malinovsky), and to the left is "Heracles and Antaeus" (1809–1811, sculptor: Stepan Pimenov). The nature of the plastic

**39**
Mining Institute. 1806–1811, architect: Andrei Voronikhin

**40**
St Andrew's Cathedral
1764–1780, architect: Alexander Vist

**41**
Spit of Vasilievsky Island seen from the Palace Embankment

**42**
Spit of Vasilievsky Island and the Peter and Paul Fortress

art with its exaggerated proportions yet expressive lines is in perfect accord with the heavy Doric forms of the building.
The Mining Institute has its own museum, which contains a unique geological collection put together over the course of almost three centuries. It now includes over 15 thousand specimens of rocks and minerals as well as assorted items made from precious and coloured stones. One of its most spectacular exhibits is an enormous chunk of malachite from the Urals, which weighs 1,504 kg and was presented to the museum by Catherine II.
Opposite the Mining Institute, the famous icebreaker *Krasin*, which took part in an expedition to rescue Umberto Nobile in the 1930s, is permanently anchored. Today, it is the home of a museum. The portico of the Mining Institute also looks out onto

the shipyards of the Baltic Factory, from which new vessels set out to roam the seas. On Vasilievsky Island, traditions that have come into being over the course of three centuries are perpetuated to this day. From as early as the Petrine era, Vasilievsky Island has been regarded as a centre of the arts and sciences, the permanent abode of Meditation, Knowledge and Creativity.

**43**
White Nights. View of the Neva from the roof of the Winter Palace

**44**
White Nights. Palace Bridge opening

**45**
White Nights. Lieutenant Schmidt Bridge

**46**
View of the English Embankment

**47**
Panoramic view of the Bolshaya Neva

Е БРОСАТЬ ЯКОРЕЙ

## The Admiralty

In 1704, on Admiralty Island, situated on the left bank of the Neva and bordered to the south by the Moika, work began on the building of a shipyard that was designed by Peter the Great himself. Together with the Peter and Paul Fortress, the Admiralty Shipyard became one of the city's main architectural features. In the 1730s, the architect Ivan Korobov abandoned the original plans for the Admiralty and replaced the frame-built warehouses with stone buildings. Moreover, he masterminded the construction of a tower with a tall gilded spire (72 m high) topped with a weather vane in the shape of a three-sailed frigate. At the beginning of the 19th century, the Admiralty underwent fundamental reconstruction under the watchful eye of Andrean Zakharov. The Classical architect, while preserving Korobov's original concept, considerably enlarged the building and enhanced its appearance using sculptural designs. The New Admiralty was envisaged as a unique monument to the Russian fleet, thus its main entrance was given the form of a triumphal arch. Zakharov repeated the motif of the wide archway in the façades of the two symmetrically placed pavilions that face the Neva.
The sculptural embellishments that indicate the purpose served by the Admiralty play an important part in the composition of the building as a whole. The idea of the synthesis of architecture and sculpture was central to Classical design and was first clearly demonstrated in Andrean Zakharov's work. He presented sculpture in all its manifestations, from freestanding statues to sculpted ornament, united by a single theme – the glorification of Russia's naval prowess.
In front of the main entrance, on either side of the triumphal arch, stand the monumental figures of sea nymphs holding orbs (1812, sculptor: Feodosy Shchedrin). Mounted on high pedestals, they are supposed to symbolise the free passage of the Russian fleet across the globe. On the attic of the lower portion of the Admiralty tower, *The Establishment of a Fleet in Russia* is depicted in high relief. Covering a length of 22 metres, this frieze (1812, sculptor: Ivan Terebenev) plays an important visual and symbolic role in the décor of the building. Statues of ancient mythological and historical characters look down from the four corners of the parapet of the Admiralty tower.

**48**
Central tower and spire of the Admiralty

**49**
Caravel at the top of the Admiralty spire

**50**
Admiralty Embankment
Eastern pavilion of the Admiralty

**51**
Admiralty. 1806–1819, architect: Andrean Zakharov

## Decembrists Square

From the very beginning, the Admiralty Shipyard was flanked by two squares, Palace Square on the one side and Decembrists Square (formerly Senate Square) on the other. Peter's Square became known as Senate Square in the early 19th century due to the construction of the majestic edifice of the Senate and the Synod (1829–1836).
Senate Square was rechristened in honour of a key event in the history of Russia.
On 14 December 1825, the ranks of demonstrators in the first organised protest for freedom, the Constitution and human rights lined up at the foot of the "Bronze Horseman". The insurgent regiments were gunned down and the uprising suppressed. The five leaders were subsequently executed and the remaining protesters permanently exiled to Siberia. The forms and symbols of Senate Square have become part of both the history and legend of Petersburg.

**52**
Aerial view of St Petersburg
**53**
Panoramic view of the Neva from Palace Bridge
**54**
Decembrists Square (formerly Senate Square) in winter

## The Bronze Horseman

In the late 18th century, Decembrists Square was known as Peter's Square because of the monument to Peter I (the first equestrian statue in Petersburg) that was erected there in 1782. The Senate, the Synod and the Admiralty serve as the striking wings to a stage upon which the main player is the Emperor – Peter the Great. The French sculptor Etienne Falconet's most immaculate work of art was immortalised by the great Russian poet, Alexander Pushkin, in "The Bronze Horseman". Falconet's monument to Peter the Great is the centrepiece of Decembrists Square, and its striking outline is clearly visible even from afar. The monument is a sculptural symbol of an entire epoch of Russian history. It fuses the energy and many aspects of the Emperor – Creator, Reformer and Lawmaker – into one. Falconet wrote, "My tsar does not hold a staff; he extends his beneficent right hand over the land he has conquered. He ascends the rock that serves him as a pedestal, an element of the difficulties he has surmounted".

**55**
Monument to Peter the Great (*The Bronze Horseman*)
1782, sculptor: Etienne-Maurice Falconet

**56**
Decembrists Square (formerly Senate Square)

**57**
Senate and Synod
1829–1836, architect: Carlo Rossi

## St Isaac's Square

Behind *The Bronze Horseman* towers the august edifice of St Isaac's Cathedral like a fitting backdrop. This cathedral serves as the architectural link between two magnificent squares – Decembrists Square and St Isaac's Square. While St Isaac's Cathedral was under construction, the square to its south also underwent certain changes and gradually began to take on the appearance it has today. The cathedral was intended to be the greatest in the Russian Empire. Vast amounts of money and effort were required to construct this building, which stands at a height of 101.5 metres and covers over a hectare of land. It is the fourth largest domed cathedral of its type in the world after St Peter's in Rome, St Paul's in London and Santa Maria dei Fiori in Florence. Pursuant to the Greek canon, the cathedral is surmounted with a large central dome and four smaller domes at each corner. Both inside and out, the building is adorned with sculptures and reliefs.
In 1817–1820, the magnificent Lobanov-Rostovsky residence, designed by Auguste Montferrand, was built to the east of what was then the third building of St Isaac's Cathedral. This enormous edifice in the shape of a regular triangle occupies an entire block between St Isaac's Square, Admiralty Boulevard and Voznesensky Prospekt. Its façade, overlooking the Admiralty, is decorated with a grand portico mounted on the ground floor arcade.
On the eastern side of the square, stand two buildings, the hotels *Astoria* and *Angleterre* (where the Russian poet Sergei Yesenin took his own life). The *Astoria*, on the corner of Bolshaya Morskaya Street, was erected on the site of some early residential buildings. When the architect Fedor Lidval submitted his plans for the future hotel in 1911, he was ordered to cut off a corner of the building and make it no higher than one floor, otherwise it would obstruct the wonderful view of the square that was to be had from the street.
In the 1840s the square was enlarged when the state purchased five houses on Bolshaya Morskaya Street and had them replaced with two symmetrical buildings designed by the architect Nikolai Efimov for the Ministry of State Property. St Isaac's Square also embraced the Blue Bridge, the widest in Petersburg (97.3 metres) and the former Mariinskaya Square. The appearance of the latter was dictated by the Mariinsky Palace (1839–1844).

**58**
St Isaac's Square. Monument to Nicholas I
1856–1859, sculptor: Piotr Klodt,
architect: Auguste Montferrand
St Isaac's Cathedral. 1818–1858,
architect: Auguste Montferrand

## St Isaac's Cathedral

The building that is to be seen today – the fourth to bear the name of St Isaac's – was built over the course of 40 years (1818–1858) in accordance with designs by the architect Auguste Montferrand.
Rectangular in shape, the body of the building has four columned porticoes, which make the vast bulk appear even larger than it already is. The interior of the cathedral (4,000 sq.m.) boasts a profusion of gilt, variegated marble, murals and mosaics. The best painters and sculptors of the time contributed to this unusual work of art. Central to the interior décor of St Isaac's Cathedral is the combination of coloured marbles, malachite, lapis and gilt, which creates a sumptuous setting for the many magnificent sculptures, paintings and mosaics. Some of the most striking decorations are to be seen in the drum of the main dome and the area below it. A number of eminent artists and sculptors of the Academic school of the 19th century had a hand in decorating the cathedral, including Karl Briullov, Fedor Bruni, Piotr Basin and Ivan Vitali, as well as several lesser-known masters. The mosaics inside the cathedral are particularly worthy of note. Due to the difficulty of maintaining a steady temperature within the building, it was originally planned to replace the initial paintings with mosaics. Most of the mosaics to be seen here are remarkable for their technical excellence, a fact that was celebrated at the London International Exhibition in 1862.

**59**
St Isaac's Square

**60**
St Isaac's Cathedral. Central nave

**61**
St Isaac's Cathedral. Stained glass window in the altar:
*The Ascension.* 1841–1843, designed by Heinrich-Maria Hess

**62**
St. Isaac's Cathedral. Figures of angels around a lamp

**63**
St Isaac's Cathedral. Iconostasis. Mosaic: *St Catherine*
1868–1880, designed by Timofei Neff

**64**
St Isaac's Cathedral. Iconostasis. Mosaic: *St Nicholas*
1855–1862, designed by Timofei Neff

→
**65**
St Isaac's Cathedral. Central dome

→
**66**
St Isaac's Cathedral. Iconostasis

ВОЗМИТЕСѦ ВРАТА ВѢЧНАѦ И ВНИДЕТЪ ЦРЬ СЛАВЫ

### The Mariinsky Palace

Between 1856–1859, a monument was erected to Nicholas I in the centre of St Isaac's Square. Once again, the artist responsible was Montferrand. The lamps were designed by the architect Veigelt, and the low fence surrounding the pedestal was the work of Ludwig Bonshmedt. The artists Nikolai Ramazanov and Robert Zaleman took part in the creation of the sculpture, producing the somewhat naturalistic reliefs and the female figures on the pedestal. These allegorical characters, which resemble Nicholas I's wife and daughters, symbolise the Christian virtues: Faith (with the cross and the Gospels), Wisdom (holding a mirror), Justice (bearing the scales), and Might (with a lance and shield). The model of the equestrian statue itself was made by Piotr Klodt, who personally participated in the casting of it. The sculptor's precise mathematical calculations made it possible to use just two points of support in the mounting of the horse. The resulting sculptural group creates a striking effect when viewed from any point on the square or the neighbouring streets. The masterful execution of the central statue together with the monument's fortuitous location make it a work of genuine artistic value. The Mariinsky Palace was intended as a wedding present for Nicholas I's eldest daughter, Maria. Today, the palace is occupied by the City Council. St Isaac's Square is intersected by Bolshaya Morskaya Street. Unlike the majority of the city's main avenues, the street is not straight because it follows the bends of the Moika. By the mid-19th century, many of the existing residential buildings on Bolshaya Morskaya had been significantly renovated, and by the end of the century the district was unofficially known as "the City" due to the many banks and offices located there.

**67**
Mariinsky Palace. 1839–1844,
architect: Andrei Stackenschneider

**68**
Timofei Neff. 1805–1876
*Portrait of Grand Duchess Maria Nikolaevna*
1850–1860

**69**
Mariinsky Palace. Church of St Nicholas

**70**
Mariinsky Palace. Red Room

## Palace Square

Palace Square did not gain its current title until the middle of the 18th century when the Winter Palace, the home of the Russian Emperors from 1763 to 1917, was erected along the northern edge overlooking the Neva. The Winter Palace was built in the sumptuous and ornate style of the Baroque, characteristic for its diversity, dynamism and expressiveness. By design, the palace constitutes a quadrangle with a large central courtyard. The latter was entered from the square through a pair of enormous wrought iron gates. The profusion of columns and pilasters along the façades, the riot of decorative sculptures on the roof, and the many and variform windows embellished with small pediments, combined with a generous helping of gilt, lend the building an opulent and exuberant appearance. The Winter Palace is undoubtedly the jewel in the crown of the square and strikes a somewhat "playful" chord in an otherwise austere and conservative setting dominated by the architectural works of Carlo Rossi.

Today, the Winter Palace is one of five buildings that make up the architectural ensemble of the State Hermitage Museum. Catherine II ordered the construction of a new building to house her rapidly expanding collection of artworks. Thus, the Small Hermitage (1764–1775) was built onto the Winter Palace. This building, dating from the era of early Classicism, has two façades. The main façade, which looks out over the Neva, was the work of Jean-Baptiste Vallin de La Mothe. The three-storey wing facing Millionnaya Street was designed by Yury Felten, who linked the two parts of the building by means of a hanging garden on the first floor. Further along the embankment, beyond the Small Hermitage, stands the Old Hermitage (1771–1787), also built by Felten. The name "Old Hermitage" came about in the mid-19th century after the construction of the monumental New Hermitage (1839–1852,

**71**
Palace Embankment. Winter Palace ·
1754–1762, architect: Bartolomeo Francesco Rastrelli
**72**
Panorama of Palace Square

architect: Leo von Klenze) on the Millionnaya Street side for the growing gallery, which was finally declared a "public museum" in 1852. Besides the buildings housing the museum's collection, the Hermitage complex includes the Hermitage Theatre (1783–1786, architect: Giacomo Quarenghi), which is linked to the Old Hermitage by a gallery spanning the Winter Canal.

It is generally believed that the Hermitage was established as a museum in 1764, when Catherine II purchased a collection belonging to the merchant Johann Gotzkowsky, which included 225 canvases by renowned Western European masters. Today, the Hermitage collection, which has been put together over the course of more than two centuries, numbers about three million exhibits.

**73**
Winter Palace. Main Staircase (Jordan Staircase). 1754–1762, architect: Bartolomeo Rastrelli; 1838–1839, architect: Vasily Stasov

**74**
Fedor Rokotov. 1730s–1808
*Portrait of Catherine II.* Late 1770s

**75**
Winter Palace. Peter the Great Hall
1833, architect: Auguste Montferrand;
1842, architect: Vasily Stasov

**76**
Carl Fabergé. *Imperial regalia*

**77**
Winter Palace. Malachite Room
Late 1830s– early 1840s,
architect: Alexander Briullov;

**78**
Winter Palace. St George Hall (Great Throne Room)
1795, architect: Giacomo Quarenghi;
1842, architect: Vasily Stasov

## The Hermitage Interiors

The interiors of the Winter Palace, with rare exceptions, have not retained their original appearance: in 1837 they fell victim to a terrible fire. Nonetheless, the Winter Palace's Main Staircase (once known as the "Ambassadorial", or Jordan, Staircase), a sweeping, white marble affair with twin flights, still looks the way it did when it was installed in the 18th century. The monolithic granite columns, painted ceiling, sculptures, intricate stuccowork and abundance of gilt and mirrors make it at once festive, elegant and majestic.
The St George Hall or Great Throne Room was restored by Vasily Stasov in 1842. This two-tone room with an area of 800 square metres has a distinctly august and ceremonial appearance due to the white marble columns around its perimeter and its two rows of splendid bronze chandeliers. On the wall above the throne is a marble bas-relief depicting St George slaying the dragon. The parquet floor is made of 16 types of wood.
The Small Throne Room, or Peter the Great Hall, also restored by Stasov in 1842, is dedicated to the memory of Peter I. It was intended for small receptions. The walls of the room are covered

with velvet embroidered with silver. In a large niche with a rounded vault, a gilded silver throne, made in England, stands on a raised platform. A painting depicting Peter I with the goddess Minerva hangs on the wall (1730s, Jacopo Amiconi).

The décor of the Malachite Room has been preserved in its entirety. The bronze bases and capitals of the malachite columns, traced with gold, create a striking complement to the gilded doors and ceiling ornaments. The south wall is decorated with murals by the artist Antonino Vighi on the themes of *Day*, *Night* and *Poetry*. The technique used in the execution of these works was quite extraordinary: they were first painted on calico and then glued to the artificial marble of the walls.

The Raphael Loggia (1783–1792, architect: Giacomo Quarenghi) is the oldest of the original interiors that were not damaged by fire. It is covered with reproductions of the frescoes with which Raphael and his pupils decorated a gallery in the Vatican. The copies themselves were actually made on canvas in the Vatican and brought to Petersburg, where they were glued to the walls and vaults of the Loggia.

## The Pavilion Hall

The building of the Small Hermitage – the next edifice after the Winter Palace in the line of buildings running along the Palace Embankment – was created by the two gifted architects, Jean-Baptiste Vallin de la Mothe and Yury Velten. They realised Catherine's wish to have one more little palace next to the imperial residence. Such buildings, which became fashionable in the early eighteenth century, were usually erected in quiet gardens or parks and were intended for relaxation in the company of choice guests.
The décor of the Small Hermitage's Pavilion Hall combines elements of the Renaissance, Classical and Moorish styles. The interior overlooks part of the Hanging Garden that was once enclosed by a glass roof. Here, arranged around a fountain, tropical plants flourished and cast deep emerald shadows on the white marble arcades of the Pavilion Hall. The predominance of white, the splendour of the gilded bronze chandeliers with their crystal pendants, the murmur of the fountains, and the light streaming through the windows lend the Pavilion Hall an elegant and wistful atmosphere. The priceless parquet and mosaic flooring and magnificent ensemble of chandeliers make this one of the palace's most memorable interiors.
Today, the Pavilion Hall houses part of the Hermitage's collection of mid-19th century mosaic tables together with one of the highlights of the museum – the 18th-century Peacock Clock, made by the English watchmaker James Cox. In 1780, this artefact turned up in Russia, where it was bought by Prince Grigory Potemkin. The clock itself had been dismantled, and only one man – Ivan Kulibin – was able to reassemble it. This curious plaything, intended for decoration and amusement, is an intricate mechanism comprising the clockwork figures of a peacock, a cockerel, an owl and a squirrel. The dial itself is hidden in an aperture in the cap of a mushroom. When the clock is wound up, the melodious tinkling of tiny bells can be heard, after which the peacock spreads its tail feathers and the cockerel crows.

**79**
Small Hermitage. Pavilion Hall. 1850–1858, architect: Andrei Stackenschneider

**80**
Small Hermitage. The Hanging Garden. Fountain. Mid-19th century, sculptor: Felice de Fovo

**81**
The Pavilion Hall. Niche

**82**
The Peacock Clock
Second half of the 18th century. England. By James Cox

**83, 84**
The Peacock Clock. Details

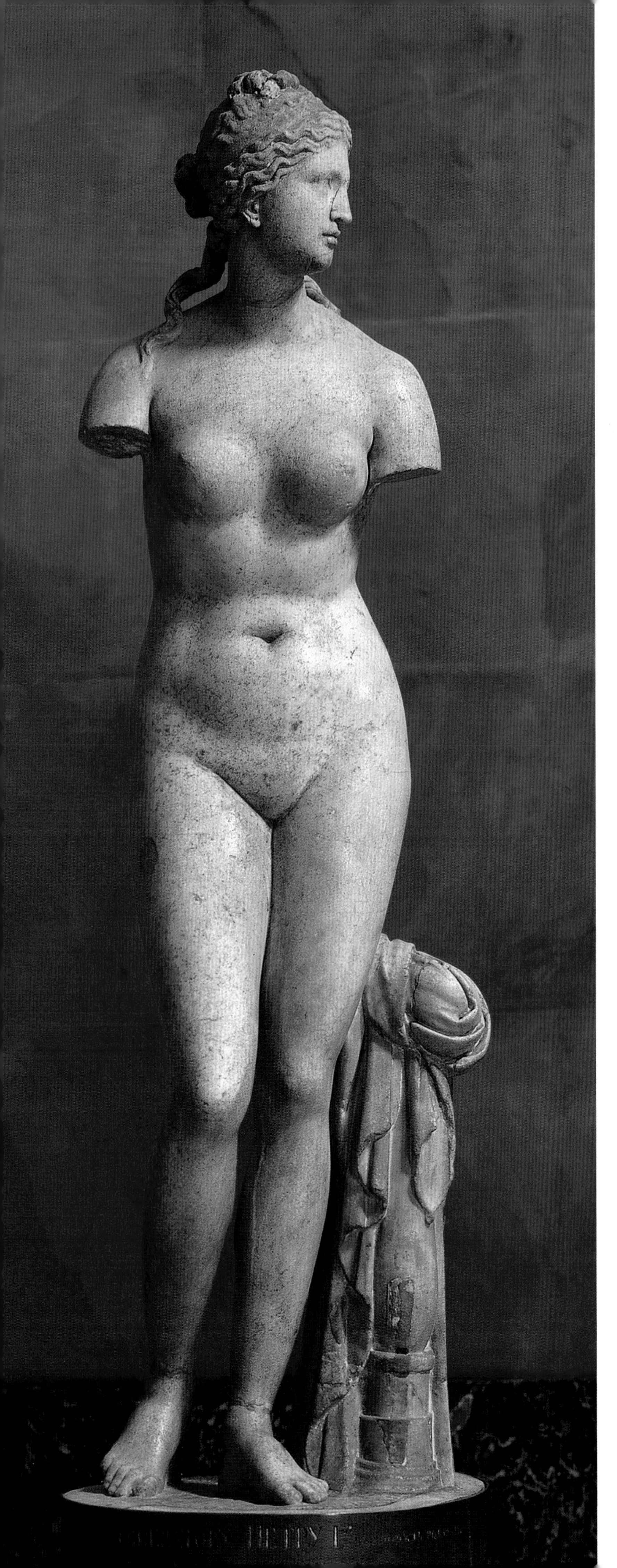

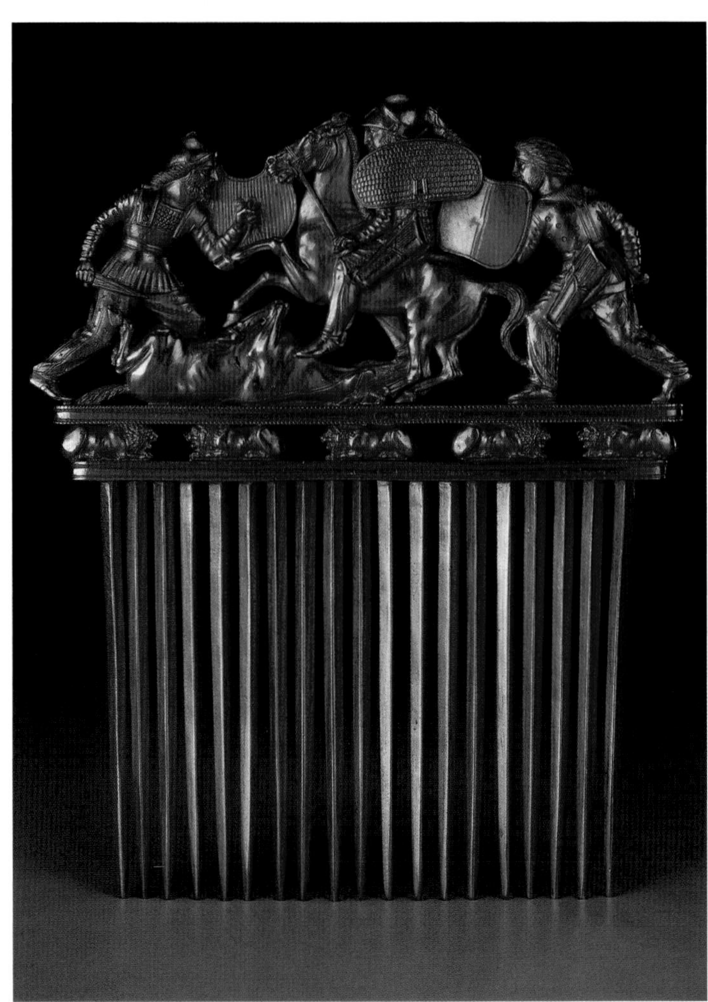

## Art of Classical Antiquity and Primitive Art

The ground floor of the New Hermitage houses the museum's collection of cultural and artistic relics of Ancient Greece and Rome, the Greek colonies in the Northern Black Sea and Ancient Italy. Its most valuable components include collections of Roman sculpture, antique glyptic ornaments, gold jewellery recovered from burial grounds on the north coast of the Black Sea, and a variety of Ancient Greek vases. The most striking embodiment of the antique ideal of beauty to be found in the Hermitage collection is the statue of the Tauride Venus, a Roman reproduction of a 3rd century artwork of the Hellenistic era (Greece). The Hermitage's Special Collection contains items made from precious metals by craftsmen who lived over two or three thousand years ago. Amongst such unique exhibits are items from Peter I's Siberian collection. These include many pairs of belt buckles, elegantly decorated with coloured paste and turquoise and depicting stylised animals mauling their victims. Of particular interest are the articles of Scythian culture dating from the 7th to the 3rd century B.C., found during the excavation of burial mounds in the valley of the River Kuban. More specifically, these are a gold comb from the Solokha burial mound, the weighty gold *Panther* and the famous golden *Deer*, which has become one of the symbols of the Hermitage.

**85**
*Venus of Tauride*
Roman copy from the original of 3rd century B.C.

**86**
Gold comb *Fighting Scythians.* 4th century B.C. Solokha burial mound

**87**
Lekythos with a white ground *Artemis with a Swan*
Early 5th century B.C. Attica. The Pan Painter

**88**
New Hermitage. Hall of Twenty Columns
1842–1851, architect: Leo von Klenze

**89**
Plaque in the shape of a deer (the Kostromskaya deer)
Late 7th – early 6th century B.C.
Barrow near Kostromskaya Station, Northern Caucasus

**90**
Old Hermitage
Leonardo da Vinci Room. 1858–1860, architect: Andrei Stackenschneider

**91**
Leonardo da Vinci. 1452–1519
*The Madonna with a Flower (The Benois Madonna).* 1478

**92**
Giorgione (Giorgio da Castelfranco). 1478(?)–1510
*Judith.* 1500s

**93**
Fra Giovanni da Fiesole (Fra Angelico). *Ca.* 1400–1455
*The Madonna and Child with St Dominic and St Thomas Aquinas.* 1424–1430

**94**
Tintoretto (Jacopo Robusti). 1518–1594
*The Birth of St John the Baptist. Ca.* 1550

## Italian Art

Although the Hermitage's collection of Italian paintings does not span every period of the country's rich artistic history, it is able to compete with some of the world's most famous Italian collections by virtue of the quality of the works on display and the renown of the men who created them. The rooms housing the Italian collection are always well attended. Particularly popular amongst visitors are Raphael's *Madonna Conestabile*, Giorgione's *Judith*, Titian's *St Sebastian*, Caravaggio's *Young Man with a Lute*, Veronese's *Adoration of the Magi* and Tintoretto's *Birth of St John the Baptist*, which are the pride of the Hermitage Museum. Without a doubt, however, two of the most outstanding and famous works to be seen here are the canvases known as *The Madonna Benois* and *The Madonna Litta*, painted by the great Renaissance artist Leonardo da Vinci.

## Dutch and Flemish Art

The Hermitage's collection of Dutch and Flemish art ranks amongst the greatest in the world in terms of breadth and quality. The first paintings by Dutch artists appeared in St Petersburg long before the foundation of the Hermitage. In 1716, Peter the Great acquired about two hundred works in Holland, which were used to adorn his residence in the capital and the suburban palaces. The Russian Tsar, as an adherent of the Dutch mode of life and culture, highly appreciated scenes from the life of "Dutch peasant men and women", according to Jacob von Stählin, and therefore superb works by genre painters such as Jan Steen, Adriaen van Ostade and Philips Wouwerman were brought to Russia during that period.
The greatest of the Dutch masters, Rembrandt Harmensz. van Rijn, is represented by 25 of his paintings, including *Flora*, *Danae* and *The Return of the Prodigal Son*. This priceless collection reflects all the stages of Rembrandt's sensational artistic career. *Flora* is a lyrical portrait of the painter's wife, Saskia, in the guise of the goddess of flowers and gardens. The artist celebrates the beauty of his young spouse, showing her dressed in a fine gown, her head crowned with flowers. In this felicitous period of his life, Rembrandt was wealthy, popular and renowned. However,

**95**
Rembrandt Harmensz. van Rijn. 1606–1669
*The Return of the Prodigal Son*. 1668–1669

**96**
Rembrandt Harmensz. van Rijn. 1606–1669
*Flora*. 1634

**97**
Rembrandt Harmensz. van Rijn. 1606–1669
*Young Woman Trying Earrings*. 1657

**98**
Rembrandt Harmensz. van Rijn. 1606–1669. *Danae*. 1636

**99**
Rembrandt Harmensz. van Rijn. 1606–1669
*The Holy Family*. 1645

**100**
Old Hermitage. View into the Rembrandt Room from the top of the Council Staircase

when Saskia died shortly afterwards, his fame and fortune began to dwindle. Rembrandt's masterpiece *Danae*, completed after the death of his wife, gives the viewer an insight into the reasons behind the great artist's conflict with society: his works were too complex, too profound and too penetrating to be understood and appreciated by his contemporaries. *The Return of the Prodigal Son* seems to sum up Rembrandt's later years, which found him lonely, impoverished but nonetheless rich in creative spirit. Here, the sentiments of love, suffering and forgiveness that prevail over all of the artist's works come to a brilliant climax.

In the 17th century, Dutch artists catered largely to the tastes of middle-class burghers who tended to decorate the walls of their homes with small paintings. Thus, the painters themselves became commonly known as the "Small Dutch Masters." The Dutch masters painted in elaborate detail, romanticising the day-to-day life of their respectable fellow countrymen without embellishing it. Works by almost all of the famous Dutch artists can be found in the Hermitage, including canvases by Adriaen van Ostade, Gerard Terborch, Willem Claesz Heda, Balthasar van der Ast, Willem Kalf, Jacob van Ruisdael, and many others. These men created genre paintings depicting scenes of the life of wealthy citizens, rustic labours, village fetes, tavern brawls and still lifes astonishingly rich in detail and accuracy as well as truly heroic landscapes. In *A Glass of Lemonade*, Gerard Terborch transforms a banal scene in a brothel into an enchanting glimpse into the meeting of two young people. Jan Steen's *Revellers* brims with humour and sly hints. Meanwhile, in his *Portrait of a Young Man*, the outstanding portrait artist Frans Hals seems to capture his subject in full flight.

Flemish painting is notable for its extraordinary integrity. The achievements and life-affirming nature of Flemish art, which is characterised by an extensive palette and an acute sense of form and movement, are essentially summed up in the works of the leading artist of this particular school, Peter Paul Rubens. The Hermitage's collection of works by Rubens, almost all of which may be labelled masterpieces, comprises over forty work, the best of which are *The Union of Earth and Water*, *Perseus and Andromeda*, and *Bacchus*.

All subsequent Flemish artists have been influenced to some degree by the great master, whose talents included sculpture, architecture and decorative art as well as various styles of painting from monumental canvases to landscapes and portraits.

Elements of Rubens' work can be seen in the paintings of other leading Flemish artists such as Frans Snyders, Anthony van Dyck and Jacob Jordaens. Frans Snyders turns the cabinet genre of still life into vast, dynamic celebrations of the abundance of forms to be found in the natural world. *Game Birds on a Table* is part of a series of four paintings that were created for the Bishop of Bruges' dining hall.

Van Dyck, the brilliant portrait artist and favourite of countless patrons, including various European monarchs, is represented in the Hermitage by over twenty of his works. His masterful *Self-Portrait* exudes elegance and artistry.

**101**
New Hermitage. Small Skylight Room
1842–1851, architect: Leo von Klenze

**102**
Peter Paul Rubens. 1577–1640
*The Union of Earth and Water. Ca.* 1618

**Spanish Art**

It was the in 19th century that the Hermitage accumulated its Spanish collection, comprising about 150 paintings. Although it is relatively small, the collection is quite good by international standards. Amongst the highlights of 17th century Spanish painting are the works of Diego Velazquez, Jose de Ribera, Francisco de Zurbaran and Bartolome Esteban Murillo. The Hermitage boasts two works by Spain's leading artist and court painter to Philip IV, the great Velazquez. *Breakfast*, the work of the eighteen-year-old painter, takes the form of a *bodegon* – a genre that was extremely popular in Spain and undoubtedly attested to the influence of Caravaggio upon his Spanish counterparts. *Bodegones* (from the Spanish for "tavern") are generally scenes set in public kitchens, the protagonists of which are Spaniards partaking of a humble meal and illuminated by thin rays of Caravaggioesque light, which pick them out starkly against the semidarkness of the background.
Francisco de Zurbaran worked exclusively in Seville, the capital of Andalusia and cultural centre of Spain. His religious paintings graced the walls of many Sevillian churches, cathedrals and monasteries. Only a limited number of works by this unusual Spanish artist are to be found outside his homeland. The Hermitage collection contains four canvases by Zurbaran. *The Childhood of the Madonna* is one of the very few small, lyrical paintings in the artist's otherwise austere and unsentimental portfolio.

Bartolome Esteban Murillo was the most popular Spanish painter amongst collectors and it is for this reason that a significant number of his works (seventeen in total) from various stages of his career are to be found in the Hermitage. *Boy with a Dog*, dating from his early period, is peopled with the lively images of the young wanderers, gypsies and beggars, dressed in motley rags yet still endowed with the capacity for spontaneous emotional expression.
In the 17th century, the art of Spanish still life reached its peak. The Spanish painters invested the objects they painted with a certain spiritual quality. One of the greatest Madrid artists of the mid-17th century, Antonio de Pereda, lovingly "explores" each object of his still life, transfixed by the transparency of glass, the solidity and colourfulness of painted ceramic crockery, or the brilliance of a metal coffee-pot. He juxtaposes the texture of each object with that of a biscuit and piece of cheese in the foreground.
The *Portrait of the Actress Antonia Zarate* is the work of the outstanding Spanish artist Francisco de Goya whose career, spanning the late 18th – early 19th century, marks the pinnacle of national art. According to her contemporaries, Antonia was better known for her beauty than her talent. She died of tuberculosis at the age of thirty-six and would most likely have been forgotten were it not for two inspired portraits by Goya. The Hermitage portrait of the actress is small and intimate. The emotional, stirring image of the young woman, described by one art historian as a "portrait of the heart", seems to represent the bridge between two eras – the old era of the great spiritual discoveries of Velazquez and Rembrandt and the new era of Delacroix, Manet, Cézanne and Picasso.

**103**
Bartolome Esteban Murillo. 1617–1682
*Boy with a Dog.* 1650s

**104**
Anthony van Dyck. 1599–1641
*Family Portrait.* 1621

**105**
Jan Steen. 1625/26–1679
*Revellers. Ca.* 1660

**106**
Antonio de Pereda. 1608–1678
*Still Life*

**107**
Nicolas Poussin. 1594–1665
*Tancred and Erminia*. 1630s

**108**
*The Adoration of the Magi*. Early 16th century
Limoges. Enamel colours

**109**
Master of the Thuison Altarpiece. 15th century
*The Entry into Jerusalem*

## French Art of the 15th–19th centuries

There is not a single collection of French cultural artefacts outside France that can compare in quality and quantity with that of the Hermitage. Many of the masterpieces to be found in the museum were acquired by Catherine II, who had the reputation of being a great admirer of French style. Porcelain dinner services manufactured in Sevres and a vast collection of tapestries, furniture and silver and bronze ornaments lend the exhibition halls a distinctive atmosphere. The Hermitage owns twelve works by the champion of French classicism, Nicolas Poussin, eight paintings by Jean-Antoine Watteau, twelve by François Boucher and a handful of canvases by Jean-Baptiste-Siméon Chardin and Jean-Honoré Fragonard. Amongst the works of the Neo-classical era are a number by the pupils and followers of Jacques-Louis David. The painting of *Napoleon Bonaparte on the Arcole Bridge* by Antoine Jean Gros gives the viewer an idea of the first revolutionary stages in the development of a "new" classicism. David's own *Sappho and Phaon* is also to be found in the Hermitage, while Eugène Delacroix is represented by two canvases full of the dynamism and energy of the era of the "romantic battle".

**110**
Antoine Jean Gros. 1771–1835
*Napoleon Bonaparte on the Arcole Bridge*
Replica of the painting produced in 1797

**111**
Eugène Delacroix. 1798–1863
*Lion Hunt in Morocco.* 1854

**112**
Dessert Service of Eugène de Beauharnais
Early 19th century. Porcelain Factory of Diehl and Guerard. Gilded porcelain

**The Impressionists and Post-Impressionists**

The second floor of the Winter Palace houses an exhibition of the main schools of painting of the late 19th – early 20th century, namely, Impressionism, Post-Impressionism, Fauvism and Cubism. The Hermitage's collection of works from this era is famed throughout the world.
It is comprised largely of canvases once owned by the early 20th-century private collectors, Sergei Shchukin and Ivan Morozov, both of whom lived in Moscow.
The works by Claude Monet, Camille Pissarro, Alfred Sisley and Pierre-Auguste Renoir that are to be found in the Hermitage date from the heyday of Impressionist painting. These artists discovered new ways of conveying the direct impressions created by natural phenomena.

They were fascinated by the effect of light on the shape and colour of objects and its miraculous ability to change both of these factors. The Impressionists fought against the rigid traditions of classical art, seeking instead to breathe new life into painting, lighten the palette and convey impressions derived directly from everyday life without renouncing the rich artistic legacy of previous eras.
In the Hermitage the paintings of Monet are represented by a number of landscapes, delightful examples of a genre that was central to his work. Although Renoir experimented with a number of genres, only his attempts at portraiture are to be found here; *Girl with a Fan* clearly illustrates the artist's heightened interest in the effects of light. In contradistinction to the other Impressionists, Edgar Degas did not paint landscapes and did not paint outdoors, preferring to work in his studio. His favourite subjects include café scenes, horse races and the lives of modistes and laundresses. The Hermitage owns several outstanding pastels by Degas, which reveal his incredible talent for portraying naked female flesh.
Paul Cézanne, Vincent van Gogh and Paul Gauguin were also active around the time of Monet, Pissarro and Renoir. Having explored the techniques of Impressionist art, they went on to develop a new style that is commonly known as Post-Impressionism. The search for new means of expression led them to an interpretation of artistic forms that subsequently gave rise to the avant-garde art of the 20th century.
Unlike the Impressionists, Paul Cézanne did not seek to convey natural impressions alone. Although he too worked outdoors, the subjects of his still lifes do not dissolve into air, becoming patches of colour, but have the same weight and substance as in the works of the Old Masters, only not by virtue of variations of light and shade, but by the alternation of warm and cold tones.
The characteristic style of the passionate Dutchman Vincent van Gogh is also founded largely upon the discoveries of the Impressionists, although light plays a more active part in his paintings than in nature. For him, colour was first and foremost an expression of the emotions that gripped him during the creative process. Essentially, van Gogh used images of the natural world as a vehicle for his inner feelings. Four of the paintings to be seen in the Hermitage date from the final and most tragic period of the artist's life.
Together with Cézanne and van Gogh, Paul Gauguin stood at the head of early 20th-century art. The Hermitage collection contains fifteen works by Gauguin from his time spent on Tahiti. Gauguin imagined the distant island

**113**
Pierre-Auguste Renoir. 1841–1919
*Girl with a Fan.* 1881

**114**
Paul Cézanne. 1839–1906
*Still Life with Curtain. Ca.* 1899

**115**
Claude Monet. 1840–1926
*Haystack at Giverny.* 1886

**116**
Vincent van Gogh. 1853–1890
*Ladies of Arles.* 1888

**117**
Paul Gauguin. 1848–1903
*Woman Holding a Fruit.* 1893

**118**
Henri Matisse. 1869–1954
*Vase of Irises.* 1912

in the Pacific as a kind of paradise where he hoped to recover the sense of harmony lost to European civilisation.

Pablo Picasso and Henri Matisse, two of the greatest artists of the 20th century, are represented in the Hermitage by some of their best works. The thirty or so paintings by Picasso to be seen in the Hermitage come from a collection once belonging to Shchukin and reflect three stages in the artist's early career: the blue, pink and cubist periods. Picasso discovered Cubism in 1906, depicting subjects taken from real life in accordance with the rules of geometry and logic. In *Woman with a Fan* the details of the woman's face and body assume basic forms combined with assorted angular shapes. Nonetheless, the unnatural geometric forms of the model's face and figure lend greater intensity to the emotional essence of the painting: the woman's pose and bowed head convey a sense of weariness and concentration. The work of Henri Matisse

**119**
Pablo Picasso. 1881–1973
*Woman with a Fan (After the Ball).* 1908

**120**
Vincent van Gogh. 1853–1890
*Lilac Bush.* 1889

serves first and foremost as an assertion of the importance of colour. In each of his paintings Matisse explores the idea that "the painter must have the gift of colour, just as the singer must have a voice." He became the pioneer of a new movement known as "Fauvism" (from the French *fauves*, meaning "wild"). In 1905, a group of young artists under the auspices of Matisse almost caused the official critics at the Salon d'Automne to explode with indignation at the sight of their bright, unruly canvases bristling with glaring colour combinations. The landscapes of Maurice de Vlaminck are harsh and dramatic. Having undergone the Fauves' "trial by colour", the artist emerged with a still greater sense of his affinity with van Gogh and Cézanne. His palette is expressive and highly charged, while his lines have an impulsive and forceful rhythm.

**121**
Edgar Degas. 1834–1917
*Woman Combing Her Hair. Ca.* 1885–1886

**122**
Henri Matisse. 1869–1954
*Dance.* 1910

**123**
Maurice de Vlaminck. 1876–1958
*View of the Seine. Ca.* 1905–1906

## The bridge over the Winter Canal

Visitors to Petersburg will not forget the elegant bridge that spans the quiet waters of the Winter Canal, linking the Old Hermitage with the Hermitage Theatre. Originally, this bridge arched so steeply that tall carriages leaned violently as they passed and almost toppled over, while in later days a car travelling at high speed would have taken off from the ground as it went over the bridge. Thus, in the 20th century, the height of the arc was altered. The bow of the bridge reflects the curved wall of the "squat yellow tower that supports the arch of the palace, from beneath which the wide river can be seen, covered with faintly whispering ice-floes like a flock of swans slowly completing their journey, and, on the far side of the river, the walls of the sombre fortress, above which a shining spire has been raised, crowned with an archangel" (Nikolai Antsiferov).

**124**
View of the Hermitage complex from the Palace Bridge

**125**
Winter Canal

**126**
New Hermitage. Portico with Atlantes. 1848,
architect: Leo von Klenze, sculptor: Alexander Terebenev

## The New Hermitage

The New Hermitage occupies a special place amongst the various buildings comprising the museum. It owes its existence to Nicholas I, who recognised the need for premises specifically designed to house the crown treasures, which had previously been scattered amongst various palaces throughout the capital. Emperor Nicholas I entrusted the "Imperial Museum" project to the Bavarian King Ludwig I's court architect, Leo von Klenze, who created this unique work of architecture in collaboration with the Russian architects Stasov, Efimov and Briullov. The New Hermitage became the embodiment of the concept of the museum as a universal repository for man's artistic achievements. This idea determined the architectural design of the building, the first purpose-built museum in Russia. In accordance with the Emperor's wishes, all the rooms of the Museum, regardless of the nature of the exhibits they were to hold, were given a ceremonial décor fitting for the imperial mansions of which they were part. The ground floor of the building was set aside to house collections of antique and modern sculpture, while the upper floor was occupied largely by the various paintings amassed by the Imperial Court. Everything within its walls was arranged according to a specific system with the sole aim of creating an encyclopaedic overview of the history of world art. A museum within a museum, the New Hermitage has been preserved as such to this day and continues to present a picture of an integral cultural universe.

The rooms in which a noticeable balance has been struck between the interior design and the works of art preserved there are particularly interesting. The Hall of Twenty Columns, otherwise known as the Greco-Etruscan Vase Hall, the three magnificent rooms of the Large and Small Skylight Halls for exhibiting paintings, the Aura Room in which antique sculpture is displayed, and the Modern Sculpture Rooms are all especially worthy of note. Many of them are decorated with columns, reliefs and murals, and boast mosaic floors. The Gallery of the History of Ancient Painting is another architectural and artistic complex of the New Hermitage, besides the Raphael Loggias, in which a cycle of monumental paintings dominates the interior décor. Splendid too is the building's monumental portico decorated with the figures of ten Atlantes, each hewn from a single slab of grey granite. Carved of Serdobol stone in the studio of the sculptor Alexander Terebenev, they serve, like the ancient Propylaea, as an entrance to the Temple of High Art.

**Nevsky Prospekt**

Nevsky Prospekt, as straight as an arrow, is Petersburg's main street. Although it began to take shape within the first ten years of the city's existence, it developed very slowly because the attention of town planners and architects alike was centred first and foremost on the banks of the Neva and Vasilievsky Island as the intended heart of the emerging city.
The new capital became deserted after Peter I died, but gained a new lease of political life when Anna Ioannovna came to the throne. Building work was also revived. As a consequence of Piotr Yeropkin's famous plan to make the "trident" the basis for the layout of the city, the area between the Admiralty and the Moika became the new centre of the capital.
In 1738, one of the "radial avenues" starting from the tower of the Admiralty was officially christened "Nevsky Prospekt" and declared Petersburg's main street.

**127**
Singer building. Sculptural group on top of the tower
1902–1904, sculptors: Artemy Ober, Amandus Heinrich Adamson

**128**
View of Admiralty Prospekt

**129**
Nevsky Prospekt

**130**
*Grand Hotel Europe* seen from the balcony of Gostiny Dvor

**131**
View of Nevsky Prospekt
and Griboedov Canal from Kazan Cathedral.
Singer building (House of Books)
1902–1904, architect: Pavel Suzor

ПАССАЖ
СЕВЕР
РЕСТОРАН

HOTEL EUROPE

КНИГИ

## The Cathedral of the Kazan Icon of the Mother of God (Kazan Cathedral)

On Nevsky Prospekt only a very few 18th-century buildings are to be seen in their original guise, one of which stands on the corner of the Moika beside the Green Bridge. The Stroganov Palace (1752–1754) is one of the few examples of the private residences designed by Rastrelli. The then huge three-storey palace is a reminder of the splendour of Elizabeth Petrovna's reign and the inordinate wealth of the Stroganovs, who owned "half of the Urals" and 25,000 serfs. The owner of the palace, Alexander Sergeevich, received an excellent technical education abroad and, while travelling around Italy, became fascinated by the arts and began to purchase a variety of works. He built up an extensive collection of paintings, engravings, coins and items of applied art. Having significant resources at his disposal, Stroganov also sponsored writers, musicians and poets, one of them a young man by the name of Andrei Voronikhin from one of the families in bondage to his father. Voronikhin later designed the Cathedral of the Kazan Icon of the Mother of God, which stands a short distance away from the Stroganov Palace.
The cathedral was named in honour of the holy Kazan Icon of the Mother of God, one of the precious relics of the Russian Orthodox Church that is kept there. Since the cathedral was constructed between 1801–1811, during the time of the Napoleonic campaigns, it became a unique monument to the valour of the Russian army. Field Marshal Mikhail Kutuzov, the man who led the army that defeated Napoleon in 1812, is buried inside the cathedral. Standards seized from enemy armies decorate the walls. The ensemble of the square is completed by two statues by Boris Orlovsky, erected in front of the cathedral in 1832. These are monuments to Field Marshals Kutuzov and Mikhail Barclay de Tolly, heroes of 1812. The colonnade that conceals the main bulk of the Cathedral of the Kazan

Icon of the Mother of God lends the entire building an unusual combination of gracefulness and majesty. The monumental portals at either end resemble vast gateways. The elegance and august simplicity of the interior of the cathedral is also quite stunning. A pair of colonnades divides the interior into three naves, giving it the secular appearance of a room in a palace. The longest and widest

**132**
Kazan Cathedral. 1801–1811, architect: Andrei Voronikhin

**133**
Kazan Cathedral. North chapel
Tomb of Field Marshal Mikhail Kutuzov

**134**
Kazan Cathedral. Interior

**135**
Kazan Cathedral. Kazan Icon of the Mother of God

of these is the central nave. Above the point at which the central nave meets the transept towers the dome, the first in Russia to be built using metal supports. The light flooding in through the windows of the dome makes the cathedral seem very spacious. Monumental sculpture plays an important part in the building's décor, including the large statues in the porticoes and countless reliefs. The monolithic columns of porphyry, with their exquisite bases and capitals traced in bronze, give the interior an air of formal grandeur just as the architect had intended. The best sculptors and painters were enlisted to decorate the Kazan Cathedral and transformed it into a "temple of Russian art". For several decades, the building was occupied by the Museum of Religion and Atheism. Consequently, only a few icons and precious artefacts remained within its walls. Now that the cathedral has been returned to the bosom of the Church, it has once again acquired a wealth of items for use in religious ceremony.

## "Antique" bridges

Petersburg has more bridges than any other city in the world, including Venice, Amsterdam and Stockholm. Today, over three hundred bridges link the forty-two islands that make up Petersburg. Together with the magnificent architectural ensembles, the bridges play an important part in the general makeup of the city. Petersburg can be called a unique museum of bridges. These indispensable structures are not only fine examples of technical achievement, but also works of art in their own right, which reflect the tastes of the various eras. There is a distinct contrast, for example, between the Trinity Bridge with its steel supports concealed by the graceful, fluid lines of the Art Nouveau style, and the Peter the Great (or Bolsheokhtinsky) Bridge with its "bulky, coarse and obtrusive" design.

Nevsky Prospekt intersects a number of rivers and canals. The bridges spanning these are a characteristic feature of Petersburg. The city boasts a number of "antique" bridges, which have maintained their original appearance. These are to be found in the centre of the northern capital, joining the banks of the former Krivusha River. At the time of Catherine II, the river was lined with granite and named the Catherine Canal. The latter runs resolutely between plain streets and gloomy buildings, while the ghosts of Nikolai Gogol and Fedor Dostoevsky's heroes seem to haunt the narrow, dark, stone passageways and roam the countless courtyards on either side. Now known as Griboedov Canal, the river makes its way beneath an incredible number of bridges. Of all twenty of these, the most striking are the Lion Bridge and the Bank Bridge (both built in 1825–26), which owe their unique appearance and fantastic ornaments to the architect Wilhelm Traitteur and the sculptor Pavel Sokolov. Bank Bridge, a pedestrian suspension bridge that is the narrowest in the city (1.85 metres), is situated in front of the former Assignment Bank (now occupied by the University of Economics and Finance). At either end sit pairs of griffins – mythical creatures in the form of winged lions. Stories and legends describe these beasts as reliable guardians of treasure, making them an apt choice for this particular location.

**136**
Kazan Cathedral

**137**
Monument to Field Marshal Mikhail Barclay de Tolly
1837, sculptor: Boris Orlovsky

**138**
Griboedov Canal. Bank Bridge. 1825–1826, engineer: Wilhelm Traitteur, sculptor: Pavel Sokolov

**139**
Bank Bridge. Griffins

## Pushkin's Apartment

A number of well-preserved private residences dating from the late 18th – early 19th century line the banks of the Moika River. Amongst them is one that is particularly dear to all Russians, for it is inseparably linked with the name of the great national poet Alexander Pushkin. Here, in the house belonging to Princess Volkonskaya, Pushkin made his final home, where he lived with his family from November 1836 until his death on 29 January 1837. It is to this place that he was brought, mortally wounded, following his fatal duel with Georges d'Anthès, the adopted son of the Dutch ambassador. And it is to this place that representatives of all walks of local society thronged during Pushkin's tragic last hours, united by their grief.

**140**
View of the Pushkin Memorial Museum at 12, Moika River Embankment

**141**
Pushkin Memorial Museum. Drawing room

**142**
Orest Kiprensky. *Portrait of Alexander Pushkin.* 1827

**143**
Alexander Briullov. *Portrait of Natalia Pushkina.* 1832

**144**
Pushkin Memorial Museum. The poet's study

## The Russian Museum

Mikhailovskaya Street joins Nevsky Prospekt with Arts Square (formerly Mikhailovskaya Square), the product of an ingenious piece of urban design by Carlo Rossi. The architectural centrepiece of the square was the Mikhailovsky Palace (1819–1825), named after its owner, Grand Duke Mikhail Pavlovich, the younger brother of Alexander I and Nicholas I. The design of the palace façade that overlooks the Mikhailovsky Garden emphasises the link with the natural landscape. On the ground floor, an open terrace with a flight of steps forms the exit into the park. Arts Square is a monument to the Pushkin era, the "Golden Age" of Russian culture. Hence, a statue of Pushkin was erected in the centre of the square in 1957, the work of the famous and talented sculptor Mikhail Anikushin. In 1895, the Mikhailovsky Palace was purchased by the state to house the first state museum of national art. In conjunction with this, fundamental alterations were made to the palace interiors. Thus, only a small number of these have retained their original appearance. The Vestibule and the Main Staircase, for example, have barely changed. The most interesting room, however, is the White Hall, where not only the colourful murals, but also the furniture designed by Rossi have been preserved. On 13 April 1895, Emperor Nicholas II signed Imperial Decree No. 420 "On the foundation of the special establishment called 'The Russian Museum of Emperor Alexander III' and on allotting the Mikhailovsky Palace with all its wings, services and garden for this purpose." Three years later, on 7 March 1898, the doors of the Mikhailovsky Palace in St Petersburg were opened to visitors to the first state museum of national fine arts in Russia. While the museum was recently celebrating its centenary, it also underwent great changes. The museum boasts about 400,000 exhibits – paintings, drawings, sculptures, objects of folk and applied arts. Nowadays it occupies four beautiful palaces in the centre of St Petersburg – the Mikhailovsky Palace, the Stroganov Palace, the Marble Palace and the Engineers' Castle.

**145**
Portico of the Russian Museum

**146**
Unknown artist
*Portrait of Alexander III.* 1880–1890

**147**
Russian Museum. Large Academic Hall. 1999

**148**
Russian Museum. Upper landing of the Main Staircase
1819–1825, architect: Carlo Rossi

**149**
Russian Museum. White Hall. 1819–1825, architect: Carlo Rossi
**150**
Russian Museum. Icon: *St George and the Dragon.* 15th century

## Art of Ancient Russia

The Russian Museum has lately accumulated a significant collection of early Russian artworks. These include such priceless icons as *The Angel with the Golden Hair* and *St George and the Dragon*. The first of these is one of the most famous depictions of the Archangel Gabriel, showing the obedient servant of God delivering his message to the Virgin at the Annunciation. The icon of the archangel would once have been found on the central row of an iconostasis, on which Biblical figures were depicted by rank. The Archangels and Angels were considered the highest ranking of the nine "choirs" of supernatural beings that performed the will of God and played a part in the lives of men. St George is one of the most revered and well-loved of the saints in Russia. One of the most popular tales celebrating the miraculous strength of this man who lived in the 3rd century AD is that of *St George and the Dragon*, which, like so many mythological and folk stories, tells of a heroic individual vanquishing a monster. This is one type of iconographic image in which the idea of St George attaining his might by virtue of his faith is particularly apparent. Against a scarlet background (the "colour of eternity"), a youthful, beardless rider gallops on a white horse. In his right hand he holds a lance with which he pierces the evil snake. The young man's visage expresses peace and radiant hope. Worship of St George became an integral part of early Russian culture and numerous monasteries and churches were erected in his honour. The image of the saint was first incorporated into the coat of arms of Moscow and later became a symbol of the entire early Russian state.

**151**
Icon: *The Archangel Gabriel* (*The Angel with the Golden Hair*). 12th century
**152**
View of the Academic Room (Room 15)

## From Academic painting to the avant-garde

The museum officially opened in 1895. At the time, it contained 445 paintings, which were taken from the Academy of Arts Museum, the Hermitage and other palace collections. Thus, the Hermitage contributed the world-famous illustration of *The Last Day of Pompeii* by Karl Briullov, the huge canvas depicting *The Brazen Serpent* by Fedor Bruni, and Ivan Aivazovsky's most celebrated seascape, *The Tenth Wave*. These works were to be seen in the large rooms devoted to Academic painting. Here too, exhibits from the Academy of Arts Museum were displayed, including student "programmes" and Diploma Works, such as those of Alexander Ivanov. Ivanov's painting *Christ's Appearance before the People* is an epoch-making landmark in the history of Russian art. It took the artist more than thirty years to complete it – he practically worked on it throughout his entire artistic career. The painting is based on the Romantic idea of a sudden awareness. While implementing his concept, Ivanov chose a symbolic episode from the history of mankind – the moment of Christ's appearance before the people, the turning of a myth into reality – which might be interpreted in a number of ways. It was precisely the various "states" and moods of the people in connection with the appearance of Jesus Christ that Ivanov sought so hard

**153**
Karl Briullov. 1799–1852. *Portrait of the Shishmarev Sisters.* 1839

**154**
Karl Briullov. 1799–1852. *The Last Day of Pompeii.* 1833

**155**
Ivan Aivazovsky. 1817–1900. *The Tenth Wave.* 1850

**156**
Vasily Surikov. 1848–1916. *Taking of a Snow Fortress.* 1891

and long to convey. The version of *Christ's Appearance before the People* that can be seen in the Russian Museum is a large sketch which preceded the final variant of the painting, now in the Tretyakov Gallery. Alexander Ivanov painted his work in Italy during the 1820s and early 1850s. An entire series of splendid large-scale portraits by Karl Briullov, otherwise known as "the great Karl", hangs in the Russian Museum. Gogol once wrote that, "his works are perhaps the first to be accessible to everyone with their liveliness and pure mirror images of nature. His works are the first that even an artist with a highly developed sense of taste but no knowledge of art can understand (yet not all alike). They are the first to have the enviable fate of enjoying world-wide acclaim, and the most highly reputed of these to this day is *The Last Day of Pompeii*, which because of its unusual breadth and embrace of all things beautiful, may perhaps be compared to an opera, if only for the fact that opera is the conjunction of the threefold world of art: painting, poetry and music. Briullov's paintings may be called complete, universal creations. They combine all things".
The gems of the exhibit included canvases by Ivan Kramskoy, Nikolai Gay, Ivan Shishkin, Vasily Surikov and Mikhail Vrubel. One of the most popular figures among the Russian artists of the late 19th – early 20th century was Ilya Repin. His art is represented in the Russian Museum by many works from various periods beginning with his earliest essays as an artist. One of the greatest achievements of his artistic career is the picture *The Zaporozhye Cossacks*, painted between 1880 and 1891. The Russian Museum owns the world's best collection of works by the Russian avant-garde artists, including such internationally acclaimed painters as Wassily Kandinsky, Kasimir Malevich and Pavel Filonov. Kandinsky was the founder of abstract painting, the first to find new ways of expressing the spiritual side of human existence and of liberating art from the study of objects by exploring the vibrancy and expressiveness of colour and rhythm. The Petersburg artist Filonov developed

**157**
Ilya Repin. 1844–1930
*The Zaporozhye Cossacks*. 1880–1891

**158**
Ivan Shishkin. 1832–1898
*Mast-Tree Grove*. 1898

**159**
Nikolai Roerich. 1874–1947
*Guests from Overseas*. 1902

his own technique of "analytical art". His works organically combine the objective and the subjective, the rational and the intuitive. The objective world, when subjected to the analysis of the brush, is transformed into a picture of the universal, of that which is conceived by the energy of the Creator. Malevich, having studied Impressionism and Cubism, completed the transition to formlessness by "inventing" Suprematism – a variety of geometric abstraction. Suprematism, in the artist's own words, can be divided into three stages represented by an equal number of squares, black, red and white. "The basis for their construction was an essential economical principle, i.e., to convey the power of statics or of visible, dynamic peace in one dimension."

**160**
Liubov Popova. 1889–1924. *Man+Air+Space*

**161**
Kasimir Malevich. 1878–1935
*Portrait of a Woman. Ca.* 1930

**162**
Kasimir Malevich. 1878–1935. *Red Cavalry.* 1918

**163**
Wassily Kandinsky. 1866–1944. *Twilight.* 1917

**164**
Monument to Catherine II. 1873, designed by Mikhail Mikeshin, sculptors: Alexander Opekushin, Matvei Chizhov

**165, 166**
Monument to Catherine II. Details of the pedestal: Alexander Bezborodko and Ivan Betskoi; Grigory Potemkin and Alexander Suvorov

**167**
Architect Rossi Street

**168**
Alexandrinsky Theatre
1828–1832, architect: Carlo Rossi

**169**
Yeliseev's shop
1902–1903, architect: Gavriil Baranovsky

### Ostrovsky Square and the Yeliseev's shop

The entire architectural ensemble of Ostrovsky Square, which opens out onto Nevsky Prospekt, and the street that links it to another smaller plaza now known as Lomonosov Square, became one of Rossi's greatest masterpieces of urban design.

The humble task of building the Alexandrinsky Theatre evolved into a fantastic plan to create an entire block. To begin with, two small pavilions (1817–1818), linked by a beautiful fence, appeared on the eastern side of the square. They served as the arsenal of the Anichkov Palace (1741–1750s), a building that a number of architects had a hand in, including Rastrelli. The palace was built for Elizabeth Petrovna, who presented it to her favourite and, as legend has it, morganatic husband, Count Alexei Razumovsky. Before the October Revolution of 1917, it was the site of one of the imperial residences.

The main component of the Ostrovsky Square ensemble, the Alexandrinsky Theatre, was erected in 1832, and is now an outstanding monument to Russian Classicism.

In 1873, a monument to Catherine II was erected in the centre of the square. At the feet of the towering Empress sit eminent figures of her time, including dignitaries, military leaders, scientists and artists.

Besides Gostiny Dvor, there is another no less famous emporium on Nevsky Prospekt, at the junction with Malaya Sadovaya Street. This belonged to one of the representatives of a famous dynasty of merchants,Yeliseev. Today, the building that houses the Yeliseev's shop is also the home of the Akimov Comedy Theatre.

**170**
Eagle. Railings of the square in front of the Anichkov Palace

**171, 173**
Anichkov Bridge
Sculptural groups: *The Taming of the Horse*
1841–1850, sculptor: Piotr Klodt

**172**
Rossi Pavilion. 1817–1818, architect: Carlo Rossi

**174**
Anichkov Bridge.1785, engineers: Johann Gerard, Piotr Sukhtelen; 1841, engineer: Ivan Butats; architect: Alexander Briullov (railings)

### The Anichkov Bridge

Built at Peter I's behest in 1715 on the main road that joined the capital with the outlying villages, the Anichkov Bridge was one of the first bridges in Petersburg. Over the years, the appearance of the Anichkov Bridge has changed several times in accordance with the type of building materials used.
In 1841, it finally acquired the appearance it has today. It was rebuilt in stone in just six months, a record-breaking achievement at the time. The principal feature of the bridge is the sculptural ensemble known as "The Taming of the Horse". It was the sculptor himself who suggested that the statues be placed on the Anichkov Bridge. Only two components of the original bronze sculptural group (1841) were installed: the remaining figures, facing Liteiny Prospekt, were substituted with painted plaster models since, by order of Nicholas I, the bronze originals were sent to Berlin as a gift for the king of Prussia. When the sculptor cast a second set in bronze, these too were sent abroad, this time to Naples.
Later, in 1848, once the plaster statues had been destroyed by the vagaries of the Petersburg climate, Klodt created two new groups, different to their predecessors, for the vacant pedestals on the bridge. The bronze suite on the Anichkov Bridge over the Fontanka River continues to occupy an important place amongst the sculptural embellishments of Petersburg.

## Palaces on the Fontanka
## The Beloselsky-Belozersky Palace

On the corner of Nevsky and the Fontanka stands the Beloselsky-Belozersky Palace, which was fundamentally redesigned by Andrei Stackenschneider in 1847–1848 "in the style of Rastrelli". The palace's first owner was Prince Alexander Beloselsky-Belozersky, a member of a family line leading back to the Kievan princes and the princes Beloselskie, who earned a name for themselves in the service of Peter I. This dignitary, who lived at the time of Catherine the Great, was extremely well educated and collected works of art.

The most spirited and fascinating of the prince's children was Zinaida, who became a member of the Volkonsky family by marriage. She knew six languages and was a talented writer and painter as well as enjoying the gift of a wonderful voice: Gioachino Rossini wrote a part in the opera *Tancredi* especially for her. Her villa in Rome was one of the centres of the art world, where the most colourful representatives of European culture gathered.

The last owner of the palace from the Beloselsky-Belozersky line was Konstantin Beloselsky-Belozersky. Of his children, the most famous was Olga who married Orlov, a descendent of the famous Orlov brothers. She was a beautiful woman, famed for her extraordinarily elegant and stylish dress sense. In high society, the dresses and hats that she ordered from Paris represented the very epitome of good taste. Today, a famous portrait of her by Valentin Serov can be seen in the Russian Museum.

In 1884, financial difficulties compelled the Beloselsky-Belozersky princes to sell the "family nest" to Grand Duke Sergei Alexandrovich, Alexander II's fifth son. The latter acquired the palace in view of his impending marriage to Elizabeth Fedorovna, the elder sister of Nicholas II's bride-to-be. Everyone who knew this woman loved and admired her. "A rare beauty, brilliant mind, subtle humour, saintly patience and noble heart – such were the virtues of this surprising woman." Yet she did not enjoy married life with the Grand Duke, a rough, suspicious and rather cruel man, although she tried painstakingly to hide it.

The palace's last owner was Grand Duke Dmitry Pavlovich, Sergei Alexandrovich's nephew. He owes his place in the annals of history to his part in the murder of Grigory Rasputin, after which Dmitry was regarded by many as a national hero. After the Revolution, he resurfaced in France, where he met Coco Chanel and even became her lover for a time. Dmitry died in 1942 in Davos.

Today, the Beloselsky-Belozersky Palace is the home of the City Cultural Centre. This organisation strives to preserve the artistic atmosphere that once prevailed within the building's walls.

## The Sheremetev Palace (Fountain House)

The palaces of Petersburg often face the water. A particularly large number of them are to be found on the banks of the Fontanka River. As a rule, in the 18th century, they were part of the large estates and gardens that overlooked either Sadovaya Street or Liteiny Prospekt. By the beginning of the 20th-century, however, the gardens had largely disappeared. An excellent example of 18th century design to be found today is the so-called "Fountain House", once the home of the Sheremetev family. In 1712, Peter the Great himself presented Boris Sheremetev with a plot of land on the banks of the Fontanka River. Here, Sheremetev built a small wooden mansion, which his son, Peter, replaced with a two-storey stone palace in the 1750s. In its basic design and external appearance, the seat of the Sheremetevs resembles other palatial residences built on the banks of the Fontanka in the first half of the 18th century. The style of the Fountain House's main façade

**175**
Beloselsky-Belozersky Palace
1847–1848, architect: Andrei Stackenschneider

**176**
Grand Duchess Elizabeth Fedorovna. Photograph

**177**
Beloselsky-Belozersky Palace
View from the window of the Gold Drawing Room

**178**
Sheremetev Palace. 1746–1750, architects: Savva Chevakinsky, Fedor Argunov

**179**
Sheremetev family coat of arms on the gateway

is typical of palace architecture of the mid-18th century. The central section is surmounted with an arched frontispiece, while the side wings are decorated with pilasters and topped with pediments. The interior of the palace was refashioned a number of times by such outstanding architects as Starov, Quarenghi and Voronikhin. The front of the building is crowned with a coat-of-arms bearing the slogan *Deus conservat omnia* (God protects all). In 1867, the architect Nikolai Benois separated the main courtyard from the embankment with wrought iron railings and gates with Baroque motifs.
Certain inhabitants of the Fountain House have left a lasting mark on the history of Russian culture. In the 18th – early 19th century, the Sheremetev family maintained a splendid serf theatre in the Kuskovo and Ostankino estates in the suburbs of Moscow, which rivalled the best European theatres in terms of its organisational flair and the professionalism and artistry of its actors. The theatre's leading actress and singer was Praskovia Zhemchugova, whose family was in bondage to the Sheremetevs.
In 1801, however, she married Nicholas Sheremetev and became a countess. She spent her final years in the Fountain House, where she died in 1804 three weeks after the birth of her son. The count passed away in 1809, and their child, Dmitry, became the sole heir to the Sheremetev estate. Unlike his parents, he had no talent or passion for the theatre, although he did inherit their love of music and the arts. His choir, whose concerts were attended by the most eminent of guests, was renowned throughout Petersburg. The count also patronised various artists, the most famous of whom, Orest Kiprensky, painted a portrait of Pushkin in the Fountain House.

In the early 20th century, Poetry herself took up residence in the Fountain House in the guise of Anna Akhmatova. The palace, filled with the memory of its owners and guests, served Akhmatova both as a home and a source of inspiration.

### The Shuvalov Palace

A little further down on the right-hand bank of the Fontanka, not far from the Anickov Bridge, stands the palace of the Naryshkin-Shuvalov family. In 1799, the residence became the property of a member of the ancient Russian line of the Naryshkins, Dmitry Lvovich. His wife, Maria, was a woman of incredible beauty and even Alexander I, the heir apparent, could not resist her charms. The two fell in love and had children, of whom Sofia was her father's favourite. Her premature death in 1824 affected Alexander profoundly: "She is dead. I am punished for all my sins."
The home of the Naryshkins with its splendid drawing rooms and vast Alexander Hall became famous for balls and concerts. In 1838,

**180**
Shuvalov Palace. 1844–1846, architects: Bernard Simon, Nikolai Efimov

**181**
Shuvalov Palace. Main Staircase

**182**
Shuvalov Palace. Blue Drawing Room

**183**
Fontanka River Embankment
Holy Trinity (Izmailovsky) Cathedral

**184**
Fontanka River Embankment.
The Karlova Residence (centre). 1790s; 1843, architect: Wilhelm Langwagen

the palace passed to Dmitry's nephew, Lev Alexandrovich Naryshkin. In 1846, his daughter married Piotr Shuvalov, and the palace subsequently underwent significant changes masterminded by the Swiss architect, Bernard Simon. The palace's most interesting features include the vestibule and the main staircase with its first-floor colonnade, the Gold Drawing Room and the Blue and Red Drawing Rooms. In the Gold Drawing Room Simon used a highly intricate motif of carved wooden columns, the spiralling forms of which frame the doors and windows. These are adorned with gilded Cupids and support heavy, elaborate Baroque pediments. The peaked ceiling is decorated with ornamental plasterwork and murals. For the Red Drawing Room, crowned with a semicircular vault, Simon chose dark polished walnut. Gothic motifs can be seen in the Knights Hall, which is decorated with a plaster frieze depicting scenes of a medieval tournament.
After the Great October Revolution, the Shuvalov Palace became the home of the Museum of Domestic Life. The exhibition included a vast array of Western European paintings as well as collections of earthenware, porcelain and glass. In 1925, the Shuvalov collection was given to the Hermitage. In 1964, the palace became the seat of the International House of Friendship.

**The Karlova Residence**

Not far from the Beloselsky-Belozersky Palace stands the home of the Countess Karlova, now named after its last owner. This residence is interesting not only because it is one of the few remaining examples of an 18th century urban estate: it is also closely linked with the romantic love story of its inhabitants. The Baroque façade of the building bears the coat-of-arms of Duke Georgy Mecklenburg-Strelitsky, the great-grandson of Paul I. Although he was a strict military man, Georgy was nonetheless a passionate music lover. He played the piano and the cello with great skill and even founded a chamber music quartet. It was through music too that the duke met his wife-to-be, Natalia Vanlyarskaya, a lady-in-waiting to his mother, Grand Duchess Catherine Mikhailovna. The two met in 1884 at a concert by Anton Rubinstein and fell in love at once. However, they were not to be joined in matrimony until some years later, since the Grand Duchess was categorically opposed to such a misalliance. In 1890, Georgy's parents finally gave their consent to the marriage. Natalia was granted the title Countess Karlova (from the name of the ducal estate of Karlovka near Poltava), which passed in turn to her children. In order to marry the woman he loved, the duke even relinquished the throne of the great duchy to his brother.

## The Field of Mars

In the second half of the 18th century, during the reign of Paul I, a military parade ground known as the Field of Mars was founded on Poteshny Meadow, once the site of public fetes, splendid firework displays and a large public theatre. The Field of Mars stretched for 500 metres from north to south and 300 mêtres from east to west. It was a huge open space that was snow-covered in winter and dusty in the summer, hence its nickname the "Petersburg Sahara". Along the western edge of the field ran the barracks of Paul I's Regiment of the Life Guards, who earned considerable recognition in the war of 1812. The barracks were built in 1818 according to designs by Vasily Stasov on the site of the palace in which Elizabeth Petrovna had lived prior to her ascension to the throne. The regular Classical façade of the barracks also extends the length

of the three neighbouring buildings. The barrenness of the square is softened by the greenery of the nearby Summer Garden and Mikhailovsky Gardens. The square on the Field of Mars itself came into being in 1924 after participants in the February Revolution of 1917 were buried there and a monument (the work of the architect Lev Rudnev) was erected over the graves. Blank verses by the people's commissar for education, Anatoly Lunacharsky, are carved on the face of the stone slabs of the Monument to the Victims of the February Revolution of 1917. In the 1930s, the place was transformed into a park. The Field of Mars is separated from the Neva by Suvorov Square, named after Alexander Suvorov, who is commemorated by a statue by Mikhail Kozlovsky (1801). When work first began on the statue by order of Paul I, it was intended for a different spot, namely the square in front of the Mikhailovsky Castle. However, Suvorov, a highly independent character, soon fell out of favour with the capricious Emperor, and the monument was thus installed on the Field of Mars.

**185**
View of the Moika from the roof of the Mikhailovsky Castle

**186**
Panoramic view of the Field of Mars

**187**
Monument to Generalissimo Alexander Suvorov

**The Church on the Spilled Blood (Church of the Resurrection)**

"The Church of the Resurrection of Christ on the Site of the Mortal Wounding of Emperor Alexander II" (such is the cathedral's canonical title) was built on the spot where the Emperor was assassinated on 1 March 1881 by Ignaty Grinevitsky, a member of the "Narodnaya volya" group. Hence its commonly accepted and better known name, "The Church on the Spilled Blood". The erection of churches in honour of memorable events is a long-standing tradition that dates back to the days of early Russian architecture, thus the suggestion to build a church in 1881 was immediately approved by the St Petersburg City Council. The original plans were rejected by Alexander III who wanted the church to be "built in the purely Russian style of the 17th century". He approved the designs submitted by the architect Alfred Parland and Archimandrite Ignaty (Ignaty Malyshev). It was Father Ignaty who proposed the name of the cathedral and the basic design of the building. Parland decided to use features in his decorative designs that were reminiscent of St Basil's Cathedral in Moscow, which was regarded as a unique symbol of the "national character" of Russian architecture at the time.

**188**
Church on the Spilled Blood (Church of the Resurrection)
1883–1907, architects: Alfred Parland, Archimandrite Ignaty (Ignaty Malyshev)

**189**
Egor Botman. ?–1891. *Portrait of Alexander II.* 1856

**190**
Railings of the Mikhailovsky Garden alongside the Church on the Spilled Blood

**191**
Church on the Spilled Blood. South façade

## The Church on the Spilled Blood – a unique museum of mosaics

The construction of the church and work on the décor took 24 years (1883–1907). The church is 81 metres high with a total area of 1,642 square metres. Stonecutters, artists, mosaicists, ceramists and enamellers were involved in the creation of its striking artistic ornaments. The outside of the church is decorated largely with mosaics, while the cupolas are covered with bright enamels and the hipped roofs with coloured tiles.

The 308 mosaics, with a total area of 6,560 square metres, are a true artistic and cultural treasure. Together they make up a unique collection, which has no equal anywhere else in the world. Besides traditional iconographic subjects, the coats of arms of Russian cities and administrative units are also depicted in the mosaics that cover three sides of the bell-tower. The mosaics were prepared by both Russian experts and a number of foreign firms.

Sketches for the mosaics were made by a group of over 25 artists. Of these men, we can single out Viktor Vasnetsov, who created two of the images for the interior, *The Saviour* and *The Mother and Child*, and Mikhail Nesterov, who worked on the depictions of *The Holy Saviour* and *The Resurrection* on the façades as well as a number of mosaics inside the church. Forty-two of the mosaics are the work of Nikolai Kharlamov, including *The Pantocrator* on the plafond of the central dome, which is one of the artist's most memorable works. *The Eucharist* (artist: Nikolai Kharlamov) is a liturgical interpretation of the Last Supper, depicting the sacred idea of the establishment of the rite of Communion, rather than an historical portrayal showing Christ's prediction of His imminent betrayal by Judas. In *The Eucharist*, the Saviour offers His disciples the holy bread with His right hand ("Take, this is my body"), while with His left He gives them the cup of wine ("This is my blood of the covenant, which is poured out for many"). The contributions made by Andrei Riabushkin and Vasily Beliaev to the mosaic designs are also worthy of note.

**192**
Church on the Spilled Blood
Mosaic: *Raising of a Widow's Son in Nain*
Designed by Valerian Otmar

**193**
Church on the Spilled Blood
Mosaic: *Christ in the House of Simon the Pharisee*
Designed by Firs Zhuravlev

**194**
Church on the Spilled Blood. Main altar
Mosaic: *The Eucharist*
Designed by Nikolai Kharlamov

**195**
Cupolas of the Church on the Spilled Blood

## The Church on the Spilled Blood – a monument to Orthodox architecture

In the 1830s, the Neo-Russian style emerged in Russia, an attempt to return to the Orthodox traditions of church architecture. Until recently, a negative opinion has been held of this interesting phenomenon in Russian culture due to the critical attitude of art historians at the turn of the 20th century. Many of the buildings were ruthlessly destroyed and those that remained, no longer put to their original use or bearing their original appearance, quietly awaited their demise. It is thus all the more gratifying that specialists have now turned their attention to these buildings and rehabilitated them in the eyes of both the public and the local authorities. The Church on the Spilled Blood has finally regained its good name and striking appearance. The church is both an historical monument and a work of art. The men who built it were given the difficult task of incorporating the spot on which the tragic attempt upon the life of Emperor Alexander II was committed into the interior of the church. The site of the murder is marked by a special chapel in the western part of the building beneath the bell. Here, in an area slightly below floor-level, part of the carriageway and railings that were stained with blood at the time of the assassination can be seen.
The specific conditions for the construction of the church are the reason for another of the building's idiosyncrasies: it has no central entrance. Instead, on either side of the bell-tower is a parvis with its own doorway. Inside the Church on the Spilled Blood there is not a single painting: the walls are almost entirely covered with mosaics.
Although the love of the faithful did not save the church from being closed in 1930, the will of God saved it from destruction during the Blockade when a shell fell on a cupola but did not explode. The building was further preserved by the bravery of the sappers who, under the leadership of Viktor Demidov, risked their lives in 1961 to defuse the missile. The skill, expertise and truly selfless efforts of the restorers, engineers, architects, technicians and everyone who worked on the restoration of the church have made it possible for this wonderful and unique edifice to once more bask in its own splendour and delight and amaze all who see it. In 1970, this incredible building, now a milestone in the history of church restoration, became a part of the St Isaac's Cathedral museum network.

**196**
Church on the Spilled Blood
Mosaic: *The Crucifixion.* Designed by Alfred Parland
**197**
View of Griboedov Canal
and the Church on the Spilled Blood

## The Mikhailovsky Castle

The Mikhailovsky Castle was built on the site of the wooden Summer Palace of Elizabeth Petrovna in the Summer Garden. By design, the building constitutes a square with an octagonal courtyard in the middle. The main façade faces southeast and is characterised by a riot of ornamentation. The castle was named after the church within its walls, which was dedicated to the Archangel Michael, the dread leader of the heavenly host. The building's appearance is a reflection of its owner's darkly romantic imagination. The castle was surrounded by a moat, which was passable only by means of drawbridges. Each of the faces of the building differs in its design. The façade overlooking the Moika and the Summer Garden boasts a first-floor open terrace and a magnificent flight of steps decorated with statues of Hercules and Flora. Behind the windows of the first floor lies the room in which Paul I was assassinated on 11 March 1801, in spite of the thick defensive walls of the building and the presence of the tsar's personal armed guard.

The castle served as the imperial residence for only 40 days. In 1823, it was taken over by the Engineering Academy and acquired its second name, the "Engineer's Castle". From 1837 to 1842, Fedor Dostoevsky was educated here. One of the most "Petersburg" writers, he disliked the city and its founder intensely and refused to acknowledge "Peter's doings" as the Europeanisation of Russia.

In front of the castle, on the parade ground, stands a monument to Peter the Victor, the work of Carlo Bartolomeo Rastrelli, father of the renowned architect. In its day, the model for this sculpture was approved by Peter the Great himself, yet the path to the realisation of the sculptor's plans and the raising of the monument was a long one. It was not until 1800, under Paul I, that the statue finally assumed its place.

**198**
Panoramic view of St Petersburg from the roof of the Mikhailovsky Castle

**199**
Mikhailovsky Castle. 1784–1800, architects: Vasily Bazhenov, Vincenzo Brenna

**200**
Stepan Shchukin. *Portrait of Paul I*

**201**
Mikhailovsky Castle. South façade

**202**
Mikhailovsky Castle
Church of the Archangel Michael. Iconostasis

## The Summer Garden

The oldest garden in Petersburg is the Summer Garden, which is one of the most magnificent and unique monuments to 18th-century park culture.The garden was laid in 1704.
The scope of Peter's plans for the Summer Garden was enormous. Initially, the garden stretched from the Neva to what would eventually become Nevsky Prospekt. Gradually, however, the city expanded and the value of land in the city centre increased, thus gardens and allotments began to give way to buildings.
The Summer Garden was envisaged as a "regular garden" of the Baroque era. The remaining statues in the Summer Garden (there were 220, of which 91 have survived) were created by Italian sculptors, for the most part, at the beginning of the 18th century.
The "best grille in the world" was erected along the northern edge of the garden, separating it from the thoroughfare along the Palace Embankment. The railings were created over a period of 15 years, right up until 1784.

**203**
View of Mikhailovsky Castle from the Summer Garden

**204**
Railings around the Summer Garden
1771–1784, architect: Yuri Velten, Piotr Egorov

**205**
Summer Garden. Statue of Ceres. Late 17th century
Sculptor Thomas Quellinius

## Peter I's Summer Palace

In 1711–1712, in the northeastern corner of the garden, Peter I's Summer Palace was built (architect: Andreas Schlüter, Domenico Trezzini), which, contrary to the traditions of park design, did not constitute the centrepiece of the composition, but was intended only for personal use by the tsar and his family. In accordance with the tastes of its owner, it resembles a Dutch house, and overlooks the Neva on one side and the Fontanka on another. It was possible to get to the house directly from the water, due to the creation of a small "harbour" or reservoir leading into the Fontanka. This modest house, a two-storey building with a high roof, hardly conforms to the idea of a palace fit for the "founder of the sovereign state". It is decorated simply with reliefs between the windows on the ground and first floor. It now preserves the memory of its owner, housing a museum, in which the interiors have been faithfully restored to show how the palace looked when it was first built.

**206**
Peter I's Summer Palace. 1711–1712, architects: Andreas Schlüter, Domenico Trezzini

**207**
Summer Garden. Detail of the railings

**208**
Summer Palace. Peter I's Bedroom

**209**
Summer Garden
Decorative sculpture

**210**
Summer Garden. *Peace and Abundance*
1722, sculptor: Pietro Baratta

**211**
Summer Garden. Main gate

## The Marble Palace

Petersburg's main embankment, the Palace Embankment, owes its name to the magnificent edifices that, like the jewels of a necklace, adorn the left bank of the Neva. The architectural complex of the Hermitage Museum makes up half of the Palace Embankment ensemble. The remaining stretch of the embankment is lined with palaces that once belonged, for the most part, to members of the royal family.
The earliest of the grand-ducal buildings on the Palace Embankment is the Marble Palace (1768–1785, architect: Antonio Rinaldi).
The only residence not to be named after its owner, it is a unique monument to decorative art. The façade of the first and second floors of the palace are clad in marble of various shades from all over the world. The palace interiors were also decorated with marble, but only the main staircase and the lower tier of the large hall have survived. Although the marble has faded and lost its brilliance due to the local climate, the palace is rightfully regarded as a gem of early Russian Classical architecture. The palace was first owned by Grigory Orlov, a favourite of Catherine II who presented him with this token of her "gratitude".
During a visit to Petersburg in the summer of 1776, Jean Bernoulli, grandson and nephew of the famous astronomers, wrote: "In the afternoon, I visited a splendid palace, which Her Majesty is building for Prince Orlov. Only the roof remains to be put in place. The building is decorated with marble doors, cornices and the like. The entire main staircase is also made of marble and adorned with statutes, and the walls are covered with marble slabs. It is without a doubt the most beautiful palace in Saint Petersburg, not excepting the imperial residences, although some of them are bigger."
After Orlov's death in 1783, long before the building was completed, Catherine bought it back from his successors and gave it to her grandson, Konstantin Pavlovich. From that moment until 18 May 1918,

the building served as the residence first of the Grand Duke, then of one of his six children, Konstantin Konstantinovich, who in turn had six sons and two daughters. Konstantin Konstantinovich combined his military career with the study of music, theatre and literature. Seventy of his verses, which he signed with the initials *K.R.*, have been set to music by Piotr Tchaikovsky, Serguei Rakhmaninov and other composers. The palace now belongs to the Russian Museum.

In the courtyard stands a statue of Alexander III astride a horse. This work by Paolo Trubetsky was located in the centre of the square near the Moscow Railway Station until 1936. When it was first erected, the monument aroused mixed reactions from the public. Many people saw it as a caricature of the Emperor, although the sculptor had allowed himself to be inspired by the Russian *bylinas* (heroic poems) while creating this image.

**212**
View of the Palace Embankment

**213**
Stefano Torelli. 1712–1780
*Portrait of Grigory Orlov.* After 1763

**214**
Marble Palace. Marble Hall

**215**
Marble Palace. 1768–1785,
architect: Antonio Rinaldi, sculptor Fedot Shubin

## The Palace of Grand Duke Vladimir (Academicians House)

Today, the former grand-ducal palaces situated on the Palace Embankment are mainly occupied by academic institutions. Thus, the palace of Grand Duke Vladimir is now the Academicians House. The palace was finally completed in 1872. The design of the building's main façade, which comprises Italian architectural motifs of the Renaissance era, is intended to impress. The ornaments on the exterior of the palace include 14 medallions bearing coats of arms. The grand portal is adorned with a carved oak tambour.

The original owner of the palace, Grand Duke Vladimir (the son of Alexander II) is known primarily for the fact that as of 1876, for a period of 34 years, he was president of the Academy of Arts. Of particular note are the beautifully preserved, lavish interiors, of which the most striking is the Main Staircase in the French Renaissance style. This palace consists of three parts: the four-storey main building overlooking the Neva, the winged servants' quarters facing Millionaya Street and, between them, the stables standing in the centre of a large courtyard. The main façade is decorated with sandstone from Bremen.

The Small Dining Room (small lecture hall) was decorated in the Gothic style, the variegated White Hall (ballroom) in the Rococo style, the owner's Study in the Byzantine style, and the Oak Room (banquet hall) in the "Russian" style. An interesting feature of the latter are the inscriptions of Russian sayings in Slavic lettering on the walls. Meanwhile, Grand Duchess Maria Pavlovna's drawing room was decked out in the Louis XIV style. When designing the interiors, the architect demonstrated his knowledge of a dazzling array of styles, but for all his eclecticism he nevertheless succeeded in creating a certain sense of integrity. The palace had 360 rooms in total. It is decorated with paintings, sculptures and stuccowork. Moreover, many of the rooms are hung with paintings. One of the first canvases to be brought to the new palace was Repin's *Barge Haulers on the Volga*. The owner's real pride, however, was his extensive collection of antique weapons. After the Revolution, the only thing that saved the palace's interiors and its well-stocked library from ruin was the fact that it was taken over by the Committee for the Improvement of the Living Standards of Scientists, hence its name.

**216**
Palace of Grand Duke Vladimir (Academicians House). 1867–1872, architect: Alexander Rezanov

**217**
Palace of Grand Duke Vladimir. Main Staircase

**218**
Palace of Grand Duke Vladimir. Red Drawing Room

**The Petrograd Side**
**Petrovskaya Embankment**

By the mid-19th century, Palace Square had assumed the architectural form it has today. By contrast, the city's oldest square, created at the same time as the Peter and Paul Fortress, has retained nothing but its original boundaries. To begin with, this place, which was to become known as the "Trinity Square" on Petrograd Island, was shaped by the elements, but was soon turned into a square, named in honour of the wooden Trinity Church located there. At the same time, Peter's first wooden house was built along with homes for his retinue. Of all these buildings, only the imperial dwelling has survived. It remains standing to this day, protected by a special brick shell. Peter chose the site for his first house in Petersburg himself. This small building, labelled the "Red Mansion", was built in just three days from 24 to 26 May 1703. It is the only wooden construction in the city that has survived to this day and remains standing on its original site. Its dimensions are small (12 x 5.5 x 5.72 metres), the outside walls are painted to look like bricks, and the roof is covered with shingles (small wooden boards intended to resemble tiles). There are three rooms inside in addition to the hallway: a study, dining room and bedroom. During his own lifetime, Peter I was concerned that the house be preserved for his successors

in the "distant future", thus in 1723 he ordered the construction of a protective gallery. All of the subsequent Russian monarchs, beginning with Elizabeth Petrovna, took care of this historic relic in accordance with the will of the formidable autocrat. The building's protective shell, which has changed in appearance over the course of time, has faithfully served its purpose.

Over the course of two centuries, work was carried out to reinforce the bank of the Neva in the vicinity of the building, and a small garden was laid out around it and subsequently enclosed by iron railings in 1875.

At the far end of the embankment stands the Nakhimov Naval Academy (1910–1912, architect: Alexander Dmitriev, design: Alexander Benois, sculptor: Viktor Kuznetsov), once the Peter the Great City College, where young men who have chosen to dedicate their lives to maritime service are trained.

On the stretch of river in front of the building, the cruiser *Aurora* is permanently moored.

**219**
View of the Trinity Bridge and the Peter and Paul Fortress from the Kutuzov Embankment

**220**
*Shih-tzu* statues at a landing on the Petrovskaya Embankment. 1903, engineer: Andrei Pshenitsky; 1907, architect: Leonty Benois

**221**
Peter the Great's House seen from the Petrovskaya Embankment

**Kamenoostrovsky Prospekt**

Towards the end of the 19th century, the Petrograd Side became particularly popular amongst the wealthy and influential. Thenceforth, the district's main thoroughfare, Kamenoostrovsky Prospekt, was actively developed and became known as the "Champs-Elysées of Petersburg". The image of Kamenoostrovsky Prospekt was determined in the 1910s. It was at this time that retrospection became a dominant trend in architecture, emerging around the same time as Art Nouveau. The former entailed the rejection of all things modern in favour of an idealised view of the past. Unlike Art Nouveau, it did not break with bygone eras, but incorporated techniques derived from architecture of different styles and schools, particularly the Renaissance. In the façades of Rosenstein's house on the Petrograd Side (1913–1916, architect: Andrei Belogrud) motifs from the architecture of Andreo Palladio are apparent. The corners of the main façade overlooking Lev Tolstoy Square are accentuated by protruding towers decorated with balustrades.

**Mathilda Kshesinskaya's mansion**

One of the first residences to appear in this area of town was that of Mathilda Kshesinskaya, a famous prima ballerina from the Imperial Theatres. She was Nicholas I's first love, and their relationship lasted for approximately three years. In 1900, Kshesinskaya became acquainted with Grand Duke Alexander Vladimirovich, and in 1902 she bore him a son by the name of Vladimir. In 1904, Kshesinskaya bought a plot of land, and within two years the house and all its interiors were complete.
The mansion, designed by Alexander von Gogen, served both as a private residence and a venue for the various receptions and parties held by the celebrated ballerina. Kshesinkskaya herself played an active part in designing the building, suggesting the layout of the rooms, the construction of a winter garden, and the décor of the apartments. The architectural complex of the palace included an angular gazebo overlooking the junction between two streets.
Mathilda Kshesinkskaya's house is a splendid example of the emergence of Art Nouveau in Petersburg architecture, characterised by asymmetrical designs, organically linked spaces, a range of components of varying sizes that combine to create an integral whole, and the use of stylised natural motifs.
The history of the building is as full of tragic events as the life of its owner. By a cruel twist of fate, the residence, which had once thrown its doors open to the very Emperor and many members of the royal family, became the site of the Bolshevik headquarters in 1917. Twenty years later, it became the Kirov Museum, and in 1957 it was turned into the Museum of the Revolution, renamed the "State Museum of Russian Political History" in 1991. Much of the building has since been restored and has resumed its original appearance.
The monument to the residence's original owner, Mathilda Kshesinskaya, has been reinstalled, and the museum now contains an exhibit dedicated to her.

**222**
Kshesinskaya Mansion
1904–1906, architect: Alexander von Gogen

**223**
Rosenstein's house
1913–1916, architect: Andrei Belogrud

**224**
Detail on the front of the former home of the merchant Brant

**225**
Austria Square

## The bridges of St Petersburg

During Peter's reign, there were no bridges over the Neva. The Emperor wanted the people of Petersburg, to their dismay, to share his passion for sailing, thus riverboats were the common form of transport. Peter even made it a tradition to take his retinue out in rowing- and sailing boats. Many members of his circle set out on these excursions praying to holy icons in dread of the perfidious waters.
It was not until after the death of the autocrat and "sailor" that three floating bridges appeared across the Neva. These were dismantled at the time of the spring thaws and the late autumn freezes. Only in the mid-19th century were they finally replaced with permanent bridges made of metal.
Each of Petersburg's bridges has its own distinctive structure and appearance. They are humpbacked and elegant, large and small, subtle and imposing. Their decorative wrought iron railings and lamps, coupled with the granite embankments, give the face of the city a charming and inimitable look.

Only two of the bridges over the Fontanka have retained their original appearance: the Chernyshov Bridge (now known as the Lomonosov Bridge) and the Staro-Kalinkin Bridge. Even in these cases, only the basic architectural form remains, while the technical essence has been lost. The towers of the former house a drawing mechanism: the middle section was originally made of wood and could be raised to let tall vessels pass. Equally beautiful and elegant was the Egyptian Bridge over the Fontanka. On 20 January 1905, it collapsed unexpectedly while a troop of horse-guardsmen was crossing. It was not reconstructed until 1956, this time using a different structural principle. The bridge lost most of its earlier majesty, and only the enigmatic sphinxes have resumed their positions together with the obelisks at each of the four corners. At either end of the small pedestrian Lion Bridge sit two pairs of enormous lions (2.23 metres high). In their half open jaws they hold the wrought iron rings and thick steel cables that support this striking suspension bridge. The hollow figures of the lions are mounted on the carcass of the bridge, concealing the fastenings of the cables and its mechanical framework.

**226**
Fontanka River. View of the Staro-Kalinkin Bridge. 1780s 1892–1893, architect: Mikhail Ryllo

**227**
Griboedov Canal

**228**
Fontanka River

Petersburg is the somewhat surprising home of countless lions. Made of iron, stone and bronze, these majestic creatures are to be seen on buildings and embankments all over the city. The king of the beasts has always been favoured by ruling monarchs as a symbol of power and supremacy. In the Petrine era, the lion often played the symbolic role of the vanquished: when the Northern War put an end to Swedish rule on the banks of the Neva, the lion – an emblem of Sweden – was subject to an inevitable artistic fate. Nonetheless, the mighty beast was soon reinvested with its regal qualities and took up permanent residence all over Petersburg and its environs. Pairs of sculpted lions became widespread. As a rule they are posted symmetrically at the entrances to residences and palaces, or on the granite wharves. Yet the Petersburg lion also likes to lie alone in parks, or survey its territory from keystones and attics. Once upon a time, a whole herd of lions stationed itself around the Bezborodko Villa, forming a unique fence. The lion is not perturbed by the cold northern winds or the snow that gathers in its mane in winter, despite the slightly comical appearance it gives this one-time inhabitant of the sultry wilderness. Only on cloudy autumn days, when the rain streams incessantly down its face, does it wistfully recall the hot sun of its homeland.
The early 18th century architect Piotr Eropkin, the mastermind behind the layout of the city centre, also designed the large timber warehouses

**229**
Mist on the Kriukov Canal

**230**
Griboedov Canal. Lion Bridge. 1825–1826,
engineer: Wilhelm Traitteur, sculptor: Pavel Sokolov

**231**
Fontanka River Embankment

**232**
Kolomna District viewed from the Malo-Kalinkin Bridge

on the islet known as New Holland. In the 1760s – 1780s the "geometry" of the natural channels and artificial canals was perfected by Vallin de La Mothe, who gave the entire complex a truly august appearance. The unusual beauty of New Holland captured the attention of artists and writers alike. The famous local scholar and area studies specialist, Nikolai Antsiferov, wrote of this unique work of art: "On the Moika is an island enclosed by a high red wall. It is divided in two by the canal, above which towers a splendid arch worthy of the Eternal City. It soars elegantly over the canal as if beckoning victorious galleys to pass beneath it. It stands here in a remote part of town, evidently out of place. And it seems like a kind of apparition."

**233**
View of Griboedov Canal and the Lion Bridge

**234**
New Holland. Triumphal Arch. 1765–1780, architect: Jean-Baptiste Vallin de La Mothe

**235**
Moika River Embankment

**236**
Panoramic view of the Moika River

## The Yusupov Palace

The most famous residence on the Moika is the Yusupov Palace. Here, on the night of 16 December 1916, Grigory Rasputin was murdered in a prologue to the revolutionary events of 1917. In the eyes of Nicholas II and his wife Alexandra Fedorovna, the Siberian peasant, seer and miracle worker embodied a mystic link between the Orthodox tsar and the people. Having lost the support of the upper echelons of society, the Russian autocrat hoped to curry favour with the common people with the aid of this man. Rasputin himself was aware that he was the royal family's last hope not only to stay on the throne, but also, with his apparent psychic powers, to preserve the health of the heir apparent, who suffered from haemophilia. Some were convinced that Rasputin was a clairvoyant and a prophet, the guardian angel of the royal family and of Russia as a whole. To others he was a play-acting adventurer, a perverted debauchee, a political intriguer and swindler who used religion to cover his deeds. Vexed by Rasputin's influence over the tsar, aristocrats and representatives of the royal circles alike felt compelled to take extreme measures. A conspiracy arose, and members of distinguished families, including Grand Duke Dmitry Pavlovich, Prince Felix Yusupov the Younger and Vladimir Purishkevich, a monarchist and an outspoken member of the State Duma (parliament), finally sought to assassinate the "holy man". In the palace basement is the room to which Felix Yusupov lured Rasputin in order to implement their brutal plan. Legend has it that neither poisoned cakes, nor two shots from a revolver, nor a fierce blow to the head were sufficient to kill him. It was not until Rasputin was thrown into the river that he finally died. This man and his murder are the subject of one of the last myths of Imperial Petersburg.

The first in the ancient line of the Yusupovs to own the palace, rebuilt in the 1830s from an 18th century domicile by the architect Andrei Mikhailov, was Prince Nikolai Borisovich, a dignitary during the reign of Catherine the Great. This fabulously wealthy art lover had a serf theatre that was famous in its day, and also owned a splendid collection of paintings and other works of art. He survived four reigning monarchs and was a knight of all the orders of Russia. Under Nicholas I, he was awarded with the pearl epaulette, a unique decoration devised especially for him. His wife, Tatiana Vasilievna, a relative of Grigory Potemkin, collected precious stones. Her treasures included the famous diamond known as the "Pole Star", Philip II of Spain's "Peregrine" (a pearl), and Marie-Antoinette's earrings.

The palace's last owner was Count Felix Sumarokov-Elston the Elder, otherwise known as Prince Yusupov. He has awarded the title of prince with the approval of Alexander III when he married the last surviving member of the Yusupov family, Zinaida Nikolaevna. She was very wealthy

and unusually attractive. Indeed, her contemporaries deemed her beauty "the symbol of an era". Their youngest son, Felix, went down in history as an active participant in Rasputin's murder.
The interiors of the residence, particularly the White Hall, the Ballroom, the Large Rotunda, the Red and Blue Drawing Rooms, the Turkish Study, the Moresque Drawing Room and the Main Staircase are stunningly beautiful and lavishly decorated. The unique Household Theatre, a miniature replica of an 18th–19th century playhouse, is also worthy of note.
After the revolution, an art gallery was opened in the palace, but the entire collection of paintings was soon transferred to the Hermitage and the building handed over to the Union of Educational Workers. Following the war and subsequent restoration work, the residence, which had been badly damaged by bombs and shells, became the Regional House of Teachers.

**237**
Yusupov Palace. 1830–1838, architect: Andrei Mikhailov

**238**
Yusupov Palace. Theatre

**239**
Yusupov Palace. Moresque Drawing Room

**240**
Valentin Serov. 1865–1911
*Portrait of Zinaida Yusupova.* 1902

**241**
Yusupov Palace. The Princess's Boudoir

**The Mariinsky Theatre**

The famous Mariinsky Theatre became Petersburg's principal theatre of opera and ballet in the second half of the 19th century. The Mariinsky Theatre opened its first season on 2 October 1860 with Glinka's opera *A Life for the Tsar*. Music by the famous Russian composers Rimsky-Korsakov, Mussorgsky and Tchaikovsky would be heard for the first time within its walls. The Mariinsky hosted productions by Marius Petipa. The dancers Mathilda Kshesinskaya, Anna Pavlova, Tamara Karsavina, Vatslav Nijinsky and Mikhail Fokin brought these spectacles great acclaim. The Russian school of opera also developed in the Mariinsky. Leading roles were performed by Leonid Sobinov and Fedor Chaliapin. During this period, the scenery for many of the productions was created by the artists Alexander Benois, Konstantin Korovin and Alexander Golovin, who, in 1914, designed the stage curtain that hangs in the theatre to this day. In the early 20th century, many

of the Mariinksy's soloists starred in Serguei Diaghilev's "Russian Seasons". It is here that Galina Ulanova embarked upon her artistic career. For a long time, the leading solo dancers were Natalia Dudinskaya, Konstantin Sergueev and Agrippina Vaganova.
With the coming of the famous musician Valery Gerguiev, many interesting experimental productions began to be staged, testifying to a relentless search for innovative forms in the fields of opera and ballet as well as the art of set design. The traditions of the famous stage and the rich history of expertise are painstakingly upheld within the theatre's walls.

**242**
Mariinsky Theatre
1847–1849, 1859, architect: Albert Kavos;
1883–1886, 1894, architect: Viktor Shroeter

**243**
*Boris Godunov* at the Mariinsky Theatre

**244**
*Sleeping Beauty* at the Mariinsky Theatre

**245**
Mariinsky Theatre. Auditorium

Святителю Отче Николае!

## The St Nicholas Cathedral

The area of town in which the St Nicholas Cathedral, or "Sailor's Church", stands today was once occupied by quarters for members of the Naval Department. A square that initially served as the parade ground for the Admiralty was to become the centre of this part of Petersburg and a church was erected upon it. The building project was funded by tolls taken at the St Isaac's Bridge over the Neva. The first service was held in the St Nicholas Cathedral on 14 September 1770, following the defeat of the Turkish armada at Chesma Bay. Built from 1753 to 1762 to designs by Savva Chevakinsky, a contemporary of the great 18th-century Petersburg architect Bartolomeo Rastrelli, this church is one of the city's most outstanding architectural monuments. It is remarkable for its well-preserved interior into which Chevakinsky incorporated traits of palace architecture. Following the Russian tradition, there are two churches in the cathedral. The upper, Theophany

**246**
Kriukov Canal. View of the St Nicholas Cathedral complex
**247**
St Nicholas Cathedral at night
**248**
St Nicholas Cathedral
Icon: *St Nicholas the Miracle Worker*
**249**
St Nicholas Cathedral
Interior of the Upper (Theophany) Church

Church is used mainly on Sundays and on the days of religious feasts and has a brighter, airy feel and a typically Baroque exuberance. The lower (winter) church, intended for daily use, is lit by icon lamps, candles and chandeliers, creating a magical effect. Thus, the pale blue and gold two-storey edifice with its five domes is a splendid sight both inside and out. The interior of the church is richly decorated with gilt carving, particularly fine examples of which are to be seen on the iconostasis dating from 1755–1760. Sculptures and columns wreathed with carved garlands also feature heavily in the design of the icon screen. An icon of St Nicholas, one of the most popular saints in Russia, where he is known as "Nicholas the Miracle Worker", is to be found inside the St Nicholas Cathedral. Nicholas is regarded as the saint who is "swift to aid". He is always depicted on icons as a balding old man dressed in robes that indicate his venerable status as a clergyman. His figure is typically shown full-length with his right hand raised in blessing and his left holding the Gospels. An important part of the architectural ensemble of the St Nicholas Cathedral is the freestanding four-tiered belfry, which with its beautiful lines ranks amongst the most sublime works of Russian architecture.

**250**
St Nicholas Cathedral
1753–1762, architect: Savva Chevakinsky

**251**
Red Guards Bridge in the vicinity
of the St Nicholas Cathedral

**252**
Griboedov Canal (formerly the Catherine Canal)

## The St Alexander Nevsky Monastery

Founded by order of Peter I in 1710, the St Alexander Nevsky Monastery is almost as old as the city itself. It was named in honour of St Alexander Nevsky, an outstanding 13th-century holy prince and statesman who was declared patron saint of St Petersburg by the Orthodox Church. Under his command, the Russian army triumphed over the Swedes on the banks of the Neva in 1240. Peter I decided to transfer the relics of the Orthodox Russian warrior to the new capital and thus work began on the urgent construction of the St Alexander Nevsky Monastery. In 1797, it was declared a *lavra*, the term used to describe the most important Orthodox monasteries. Within the walls of the monastery, on either side of the main entrance, lies a pair of cemeteries. To the left is the 18th-century St Lazarus Cemetery, the oldest graveyard in the city. The places of honour were considered to be along the walls of the burial-vault of the Lazarev Chapel. In 1832, the Tikhvin Cemetery was opened to the right of the entrance to the monastery. Many Russian writers, artists, composers and performers are buried here. Throughout the 18th century, many famous architects worked on the Alexander Nevsky Monastery, transforming it into an architectural ensemble that comprised buildings of different eras and styles. The construction of the monastery was completed by the renowned Russian architect Ivan Starov.

**253**
St Alexander Nevsky Monastery. Entrance

**254**
Dostoevsky's grave. 1883, sculptor: Nikolai Lavretsky

**255**
Tchaikovsky's tomb. 1897, sculptor: Piotr Kamensky

**256**
St Alexander Nevsky Monastery. Church of the Annunciation
1717–1722, architect: Domenico Trezzini

**257**
St Alexander Nevsky Monastery. St Theodore Church
1740–1750, architect: Pietro Trezzini

### The Holy Trinity Cathedral

Ivan Starov designed the main entrance to the St Alexander Nevsky Monastery, which opens out onto a square that is also his work. Starov also created the central building of the St Alexander Nevsky Monastery, the majestic Holy Trinity Cathedral, which plays an important symbolic and compositional role in the monastery ensemble. The new cathedral was built to Starov's designs from 1776–1790 in place of an existing church whose walls had begun to crack. The Holy Trinity Cathedral, which boasts two monumental belfries, is an example of religious architecture in the style of late 18th-century Russian Classicism. Sculptural panels created by Fedot Shubin can be seen

above the side entrances. Shubin too was responsible for the statues of the saints that stand inside the church. The gilded bronze gates of the iconostasis of the Holy Trinity Cathedral are of remarkable elegance and beauty.

**258**
St Alexander Nevsky Monastery
Inner courtyard

**259**
St Alexander Nevsky Monastery. Holy Trinity Cathedral
1776–1790, architect: Ivan Starov

**260**
St Alexander Nevsky Monastery. Holy Trinity Cathedral
Central nave

**261**
St Alexander Nevsky Monastery. Holy Trinity Cathedral
Shrine containing the relics of Saint Alexander Nevsky

## Russian Orthodox Churches in St Petersburg

Architectural accents are highly characteristic of the overall design of Petersburg. To begin with this role was played by the two towering spires of the Admiralty and the Peter and Paul Fortress. Later, the cupolas of religious buildings came to perform a similar function. As dominant features of the skyline in various areas of Petersburg, they played a fundamental part in shaping the appearance of the city and brought variety to the cityscape. In Petersburg, the long horizontal lines of the rivers, canals and streets, lined with buildings of almost uniform height, are broken by the verticals of belfries, spires and cupolas of various shapes and sizes. The architecture of the churches of Petersburg is magnificent. The enormous dome of St Isaac's prevails over half of the city. The St Nicholas Cathedral and its graceful four-tiered belfry looks elegant and festive from all angles and at all times of the year, while the Church on the Spilled Blood blooms at the end of Griboedov Canal like a rare and exotic perennial flower, stunning the viewer with its riot of colours and intricate architectural forms.

**262**
Holy Trinity Cathedral. 1828–1835, architect: Vasily Stasov

**263**
St Samson's Cathedral. 1728–1740

**264**
Convent of St John of Kronstadt
Main building. 1900–1908, architect: Nikolai Nikonov

**265**
Holy Prince Vladimir's Cathedral
1741–1772, architect: Mikhail Zemtsov, Pietro Trezzini, Antonio Rinaldi

Having ascended the throne, Peter I abolished the patriarchate and installed an "ecclesiastical board" known as the Holy Synod at the head of the church. This institution was overseen by the chief procurator, a lay official appointed by the Emperor himself. During the Petersburg era of Russian history, the Orthodox Church practically became a state organ. One of the signs of the Church's subordination to the state was the consecration of churches in the name of "calendar saints" who shared the names of Emperors, or in honour of saints, whose days coincided with the dates of events that were significant to the state, such as a military victory. The defeat of the Turks at Chesma Bay in 1770 was marked by the founding of the Church of the Nativity of St John the Baptist, better known as the Chesma Church. St Petersburg is also the home of a cathedral consecrated in the name of Prince Vladimir, who was canonised in the days of Ancient Rus. The Convent of St John of Kronstadt on the Karpovka River serves as a reminder of the saint who established this very institution. At the beginning of 1917 there were over 700 churches and chapels in Petersburg. Now there are approximately 100. A number of these religious buildings have now been handed back to the Church and, thanks to the efforts of restorers, their interiors have been recreated.

ВЛАДЫЧИЦА ПРИИМИ МОЛИТВЫ РАБОВ ТВОИХ

## The Smolny Monastery

The palaces and residences built in the Baroque style by the court architect Bartolomeo Francesco Rastrelli adorn the city to this day. One such work is the ensemble of the Smolny Convent situated on the upper left-hand bank of the Neva at a bend in the river. After Peter had conquered this territory, a large tar yard was built. Later, a country palace was erected here for Elizabeth and christened "Smolny" (meaning *tar*). Legend has it that in the fourth year of her reign, Elizabeth intended to hand the reins of government to her nephew, Peter III, and end her days peacefully in a convent. Cherishing this thought, she ordered the construction of a religious retreat for women on the spot where her palace stood, to be named the Convent of the Resurrection. The plans and construction work were entrusted to Rastrelli. All of the convent buildings are laid out symmetrically. In the centre stands the lofty cathedral, while around the edge of the courtyard run the living quarters with small "domestic" churches at each corner.
The Cathedral of the Resurrection in the Smolny Convent looks particularly striking both from the water and from the opposite bank. It rises up like a magical vision, sparkling with gilt and stunning the viewer with the bright blue of its walls, the intricacy of its cupolas and the beauty and elegance of its entire countenance.

**266**
Cathedral of the Transfiguration. 1743–1754, architects: Mikhail Zemtsov, Pietro Trezzini; 1828–1829, architect: Vasily Stasov

**267**
Chesma Church of the Nativity of St John the Baptist
1777–1780, architect: Yury Velten

**268**
Church of the Vladimir Icon of the Mother of God. 1761–1769
Belfry. 1783, architect: Giacomo Quarenghi

**269**
View of the Smolny Monastery

**270**
Panoramic view of the Smolny Monastery

## The Kikin Mansion and the Bezborodko Villa

The left bank of the Neva is also graced by a building that dates from the first third of the 18th century. At one time it belonged to the naval adviser Alexander Kikin, who was one of Peter the Great's associates. When Peter learned of Kikin's involvement in the affairs of the tsarevich Alexei, the Emperor dealt with the admiral severely: he was arrested and subsequently put to death. Kikin's home was confiscated, and a collection of Peter I's rarities was installed there.
Prince Alexander Bezborodko, a famous dignitary during the reign of Catherine the Great, was, according to his contemporaries, "an agile mind in a cumbersome body." For his diplomatic services, Catherine II made him one of her secret advisors and awarded him the order of St Andrew. Paul I later promoted him to the position of chancellor of state. Bezborodko was a wealthy man who had a home in Petersburg as well as a villa in Poliustrovo (now within the bounds of the city).

**271**
Smolny Cathedral. 1748–1769, architect: Bartolomeo Rastrelli
**272**
Sverdlovskaya Embankment
Stone lions outside the Bezborodko Villa
**273**
Bezborodko Villa. 1773–1777, architect: Vasily Bazhenov; 1783–1784, architect: Giacomo Quarenghi
**274**
Kikin Mansion. 1714–1720

## The February Revolution of 1917

Further along the left bank of the Neva stands a palace that was built for Catherine II's favourite, Grigory Potemkin. Potemkin was commander-in-chief of the Russian army during the Russo-Turkish War for which the military leader was awarded the title of Prince of Tauride (the early name for the Crimea). After Potemkin's death, the palace was turned into a residence for the royal family and was christened the Tauride Palace in honour of its former owner. Although the palace's interiors have undergone certain changes, the building has retained its original appearance on the outside: the central corpus, containing a series of ceremonial halls, is linked by galleries to a pair of side pavilions. This particular design subsequently served as a model for many estates throughout Russia. For over a hundred years, the palace was largely neglected. In the 20th century, however, its fate was tied to a number of significant historical events. In 1906, the palace became the seat

of the first Russian parliament: until 1916, the State Duma convened here in a room that had once served as the Winter Garden. During the February Revolution of 1917, the Duma emerged as one of the authorities in which many of those who were opposed to the imperial government put their trust. Crowds of people flocked to the Tauride Palace, entirely filling the Oval Hall, which had once been designed for balls and formal receptions but now served as the foyer to the assembly room. While the deputies of the fourth State Duma discussed the creation of a Provisional Government in the lobby of the palace, a meeting was held in the assembly room at which the Petrograd Soviet of Workers' and Soldiers' Deputies was elected. Amongst the members of the Soviet's executive committee was one Alexander Kerensky, who subsequently became a member of the Provisional Government and later prime minister. Thus, in March 1917, both the Provisional Government and the Petrograd Soviet of Workers' and Soldiers' Deputies were situated under one roof, making the Tauride Palace home to the Russian diarchy. Today, the Parliamentary Commission of the CIS meets within its walls.

**275**
State Duma in session at the Tauride Palace
Photograph

**276**
Tauride Palace. 1783–1789, architect: Ivan Starov

**277**
Alexander Kerensky. Photograph

**278**
Tauride Palace. Columned Hall

**279**
Demonstration on Nevsky Prospekt. Photograph

## The Great October Revolution

In August 1917, the Petrograd Soviet of Workers' and Soldiers' Deputies moved into the former Smolny Institute for Young Noblewomen. In September, leadership in the Soviets passed to the Bolshevik Party and Leon Trotsky was elected its chairman. Whereas the Provisional Government and the heads of the Soviets had previously worked towards a common goal, namely, the creation of a democratic Russian government, the Petrograd Soviet now assumed a very different stance, setting its sights on an armed uprising. It identified its goal as "proletarian dictatorship" and adopted the slogan: "All power to the Soviets." Preparations for an armed revolt began.
Power was to be accepted by the second All-Russian Congress of Soviets. The Congress had barely started to assembly when the uprising began. At the sound of a shot fired from the battleship *Aurora*, soldiers, sailors and Red Guards under the command of the Military Revolutionary Committee of the Petrograd Soviet stormed the Winter Palace and arrested the Provisional Government. Lenin announced to the delegates of the Congress gathered in the assembly hall at the Smolny that all power in Russia was now in their hands. The second

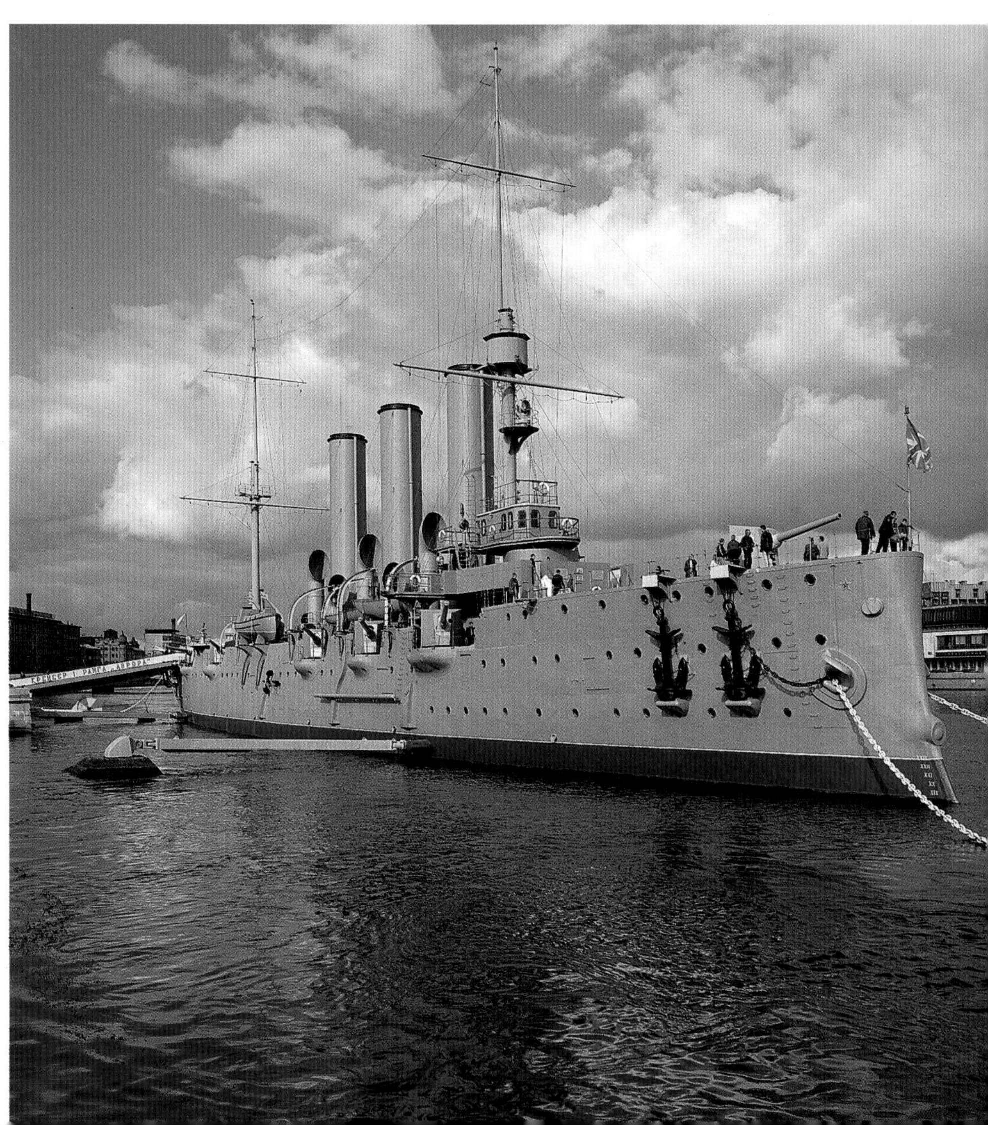

All-Russian Congress of Soviets of Workers' and Soldiers' Deputies elected the Soviet government – the Soviet of People's Commissars. For many years, the Smolny was regarded as the bastion and symbol of Soviet power. The former study of the Chairman of the Soviet (Council) of People's Commissars, Vladimir Lenin, has been preserved to this day. In 1927, a monument to Lenin (the work of the sculptor, Kozlov) was erected in front of the building's main portico, while in 1924 (the year of Lenin's death), two commemorative propylaea were built to designs by Shchuko. That same year, Petrograd was renamed Leningrad.

**280**
Smolny Institute. 1806–1808,
architect: Giacomo Quarenghi
Statue of Lenin. 1927, sculptor: Vasily Kozlov,
architect: Vladimir Shchuko

**281**
Vladimir Serov. 1910–1968
*Lenin proclaiming the power of the Soviets.* 1936

**282**
The cruiser *Aurora* at permanent anchor

**283**
Smolny Institute. Propylaea. 1923–1924, architects:
Vladimir Shchuko, Vladimir Helfreich

**284**
Smolny Institute. Lenin's study

**The Siege of Leningrad**

During the Second World War Leningrad lived through the most tragic episode in its existence, the 900-day siege lasting from September 1941 to January 1944. In September 1941, German troops were stopped short just outside Leningrad. A division of militiamen, citizen soldiers who were badly armed and hastily trained, played a vital role in defending the city, resolving to protect it at the cost of their own lives. Although the enemy did not enter the city, Leningrad was cut off from the rest of the country and the most horrific siege in the history of man began. Weakened by hunger, numbed by fierce frosts and deprived of electricity and water, people struggled to defend their native land and, with energy and resoluteness, fought for survival in the vast city. In winter, Leningrad was supplied with food and munitions by the Road of Life. This was the name given to the route, one hundred kilometres long, which linked the city with the Osinovets Cape on Lake Ladoga and, when the lake was frozen, with the eastern shore of Ladoga. The uninterrupted activity of this legendary route was maintained at the cost of the lives of numerous drivers, sappers, railwaymen, soldiers, pilots anti-aircraft gunners, and artillery men.
In January 1943, the blockade was broken on a narrow strip of the front. Years after the end of the war, the Green Belt of Glory was created on Leningrad's lines of defence, comprising approximately sixty monuments and memorials. The total length of the memorial "belt" is 220 kilometres.

A monument to the courage and fortitude of the citizens of Leningrad stands at the Piskarevskoe Memorial Cemetery. Buried here are about 450 thousand persons who perished during the siege. Over one million people died in Leningrad during the Great Patriotic War – civilians and soldiers alike. About twenty thousand persons were killed in air raids.
On the 30th anniversary of Victory in the Great War, a monument to the Heroic Defenders of Leningrad was unveiled on Victory Square.

**285**
Piskarevskoe Memorial Cemetery. Statue of the Motherland
1956–1960, sculptor: Vera Isaeva;
architects: Alexander Vasiliev, Evgueny Levinson

**286**
At a water pump on Nevsky Prospekt. Photograph

**287**
Patrol on the streets of Leningrad. Photograph

**288–290**
Monument to the Heroic Defenders of Leningrad
on Victory Square. 1974–1975, architect: Sergei Speransky,
sculptor: Mikhail Anikushin

Electroimpex
Sofia

After the war, Leningrad began to tend its wounds. In little over ten years the city was restored to its former glory: architectural and sculptural monuments were repaired, and parks and gardens were renovated along with the city's bridges and granite embankments. The celebrated palaces of Peterhof, Tsarskoye Selo and Pavlovsk were resurrected from the ruins and ashes. The city became still more magnificent and beautiful than ever. It also grew considerably and its boundaries began to stretch much further than those of pre-war Leningrad.

In contradistinction to other European capitals, Saint Petersburg has only been on the map for three hundred years. Its beauty, however, has long since earned it world-wide acclaim, and it rivals such international centres as London and Paris in terms of its fame. Tourists can often detect elements of other European cities in Saint Petersburg: its embankments are reminiscent of Paris and its many canals reminiscent of Amsterdam. The countless bridges and the tangible sense of proximity to the sea bring to mind Venice, while shades of London are to be found in the city's mists and green parks. Yet for all these similarities, Petersburg, like its counterparts, is unique and extraordinary. Even after just a single visit, it is impossible to forget the splendour of its architectural ensembles, the idiosyncratic beauty of the streets and houses of "informal" Petersburg, the ghostly charm of the White Nights, the sparkling jets of the Peterhof fountains on a bright summer's day, the gold and scarlet of the autumnal parks, or the dazzling brilliance of the winter snows.

Saint Petersburg saw in the 21st century in all its majestic beauty, emphasising its significance as a unique museum of urban planning and architecture. For the residents of Petersburg, however, the city has been and continues first and foremost to be their home. Descendants of the craftsmen who began to build Petersburg under Peter I live and work here. Through their efforts, the city continues to grow and, thus, new quarters emerge. Petersburg's commercial port, for example, receives cargo from all over the world. At the point where the Bolshaya Neva meets the Baltic Sea, the maritime face of the northern capital has taken shape. Yet no matter how much Petersburg has changed and regardless of the historical events that have shaken Russia and with it one of its key cities, the Neva River remains the same as always – a witness to human joys and woes.

Petersburg is at once united and divided by the Neva. In May, the ice floes from Lake Ladoga in the east drift past the columned façades of the city's palaces, bringing a cold northeastern wind with them. Since the time of Peter the Great, the Neva has been linked to the basin of the mighty Volga by a system of waterways. It is as if the cares of the vast territory of Russia, reaching right back to the Pacific, are carried along with the drifting ice and the winds from the east. As it wends its smooth and leisurely way, the Neva assumes a number of very different guises. From the Lieutenant Schimdt and Tuchkov Bridges right up to the Smolny Convent it is a stately, cosmopolitan river. Here, all of the architectural beauty of old Petersburg is to be seen lining its banks. Up to these bridges and beyond the Smolny stretches the working river, marked by the cranes of the freight port, the masts of boats in the shipyards and the industrial chimneys at the mouth of the Neva. By day, the Neva is quiet and majestic. Freight transportation within the city limits has almost ceased, smoky long boats no longer moor along the embankments, and the lumbering barges that once travelled the lengths of the Neva, the Nevka, the Fontanka and the Moika have given way to modern ocean liners, antique sailboats and floating restaurants in the guise of old vessels. Likewise, the so-called "water trams" that once served the city's internal waterways have been replaced by motorboats of various sizes carrying cargoes of sightseers. At night, the Neva does not belong to the city of Petersburg alone: it once again becomes a part of the ancient waterway that stretched "from the Varangians to the Greeks", linking four seas with inland Russia. During the small hours, when the bridges are raised, large ships enter the bounds of the city. The opening of the bridges begins close to the mouth of the Neva with the Lieutenant Schimdt Bridge. In front of the fifth bridge – the Bolsheokhtinsky Bridge – vessels sailing upstream stop to allow oncoming traffic to pass. They then continue on their way, passing under a further three bridges. At five a.m., all of the bridges close and once more become an integral part of the roads that join the two sides of the city. Saint Petersburg has stood out from other Russian cities from time immemorial. It owes its uniqueness first and foremost to its geographical location: Petersburg stands on the edge of the vast territory of Russia and is indeed a "window onto Europe". From the west it has not only been buffeted by the turbulent waters of the autumn floods, but also by the shockwaves of historic disasters endured on the continent, while traces of European ideas and the triumphs and tribulations of the "old continent" have been borne in on the Baltic winds.

←
**291**
Fireworks over the Neva
**292**
Balloon festival in Petersburg

# THE ENVIRONS

OF SAINT PETERSBURG

# Peterhof

No description of St Petersburg would be complete without some mention of the former imperial residences that are strung out around the edges of the northern capital like the beads of an exquisite necklace. Many of these park and palace complexes came into being at the same time as the city and, in accordance with Peter I's plans, became a delightful and fitting frame for Petersburg. Each of the country residences has its own unique and special charm and each one reflects the aesthetic tastes of different historical eras, which have been added to and altered with time. Although all of the country residences have retained evidence of the personal predilections of their various owners, the majority of them are largely associated with one or other ruler in particular. The most deserving of our attention is Peterhof, the favourite residence of Peter I, after whom it is named. Peterhof constitutes a grandiose 18th–19th century architectural and park ensemble with an area of over a thousand hectares dotted with approximately thirty buildings and pavilions and decorated with over one hundred sculptures.

**293**
Grand Cascade
Fountain: *Samson Tearing Open the Jaws of the Lion*
1801, sculptor: Mikhail Kozlovsky;
architect: Andrei Voronikhin; cast by V. Ekimov

**294**
Panorama of the Great Palace and Grand Cascade

The Emperor was a regular visitor to the naval fortress at Kronstadt. However, the path to the latter, which lay over the sea, was dangerous and uncomfortable. Thus, Catherine I, who always accompanied her husband on his travels, as legend has it, asked Peter to build a convenient stopping point on the shore of the gulf. The idea captured the tsar's active imagination and he decided to create a lavish residence. He personally chose the spot on which it was to be built and drew up plans for the layout of the park, buildings and fountains. Peter envisaged Peterhof not only as a place to rest and receive guests. The Emperor conceived it as a monument to the transfiguration of Russia, to its glorious victory in the Northern War with Sweden.
15 August 1723 saw the official opening of Peterhof. Its three palaces (the Upper Chambers, the Marly and Monplaisir), two cascades and 16 fountains left visitors stunned by their splendour. The arrangement of fountains on the terraces and in the lower park was developed and a gravity-fed water system installed in the Petrine era. At the time, these unique ornaments were given different shapes and sizes in order to achieve an array of effects with the falling water. By skilfully exploiting the lay of the extensive territory with its natural ledges, slopes and plains, architects, engineers and sculptors succeeded in creating a picturesque park and peerless architectural ensemble.
Peterhof's unique place in world culture and the significance of its fountains was once described by Alexander Benois, who wrote that Peterhof "is often compared to Versailles, but this is a misconception. The sea lends Peterhof an entirely unique character. It is as if Peterhof was born from the foaming waves, as if it was brought to life by order of the mighty tsar... The fountains of Versailles are elaborate yet dispensable ornaments. Peterhof is the residence of the ruler of the seas. The fountains of Peterhof are not an additional feature, they are its most important feature."

**295**
Grand Cascade. West staircase

**296**
View of the Grand Canal (otherwise known as the Sea or Samson Canal)

## The Grand Cascade

In front of the northern façade of the palace, stretching down towards the sea, is the Lower Park, which embraces a variety of buildings together with the Grand Cascade, two smaller cascades and numerous fountains. At the centre of this magnificent symmetrical composition is the Grand Cascade. It looks particularly striking from the water.
The Grand Cascade was first brought into action in 1723, but at the end of the 18th – beginning of the 19th century, a great deal of work had to be done to replace the damaged lead sculptures. It was at this time that seventeen bronze copies of antique originals were incorporated into the composition of the cascade. These include the *Wounded Amazon*, *Ganymede*, *Cupid and Psyche* and *Medici Venus*.
Besides the fountains themselves, sculptures and bas-reliefs play an important symbolic and ornamental part in the Grand Cascade ensemble. In the form of allegories, they represent and celebrate Russia's military prowess and naval might. The entire composition bristles with a total of 38 statues and 213 bas-reliefs, busts, mascarons and urns. The images portrayed in the sculptures and the subjects of the bas-reliefs are taken from ancient mythology. At the time of Peter I's reign, Greek antiquity in its Roman interpretation provided the chief stock of themes employed in Russian art. It was the Emperor himself who laid the foundations for this preoccupation with antiquity, and the Emperor too who acquired the first antique relic to appear in Russia, namely a statue of Venus. From that moment on, collecting antiques became a popular pastime amongst the educated nobility. Finally, the sculptural ornaments of the Grand Cascade make up a complete allegorical tale of the victories won over the enemies of Petrine Russia and at the same time celebrate the nation's entry into the European political arena.
The centrepiece of the Grand Cascade is the fountain of *Samson Tearing Open the Jaws of the Lion*, which was created in honour of the 25th anniversary of an important Russian victory. On 27 June 1709, St Samson's Day, the famous Poltava Battle took place in which the Russian army,

**297**
View of the Grand Cascade
**298**
View of the Great Palace and Grand Cascade from the Grand Canal

led by Peter I, routed King Charles XII of Sweden's troops. The aforesaid sculpture was to serve as an allegorical expression of Russia's triumph over Sweden, a task that naturally dictated the monument's design. The pious saint was transformed in the Russian interpretation into a mighty Biblical character, and the king of the beasts, which appears on the Swedish coat of arms, inevitably came to represent the northern aggressor. A twenty-metre high jet of water shoots from the jaws of the lion like a victorious salvo. The sculpture was originally created by Carlo Rastrelli, but was replaced in 1801 by the work of Mikhail Kozlovsky.

The basic design of the Grand Cascade is simple, functional and of impressive proportions. Its façade stretches for 42 metres and, due to the dimensions of the Cascade's staircase, the water falls a distance of 20 metres.

The nucleus of the Grand Cascade takes the form of the Large Grotto, faced inside and out with tufa and dived into five deep, narrow archways. The keystone of each arch is adorned with gilded mascarons. The stone bulk of the Grotto and the Cascade is set 30 metres into a slope and serves as a support for the terrace above it on which the palace stands. As in the mid-18th century, the inside of the Grotto is decorated with sculptures and fountains celebrating Russia's victory over the Swedes.

In front of the arcade of the Large Grotto, in a flat ornamental basin, play the jets of the Cascade's most complex water feature, the Basket Fountain. From a ring of tufa, 28 inclined jets criss-cross like the latticework of a flower basket, encircling eight vertical jets with a single tall jet in the very centre. The overall effect is that of a crystal basket containing delicate, pearly tulips, which flower only momentarily.

A fascinating point from which to view the Grand Cascade is the bridge across the Sea Canal that forms a link in the great alley running from west to east. Alexander Benois called this vista "classic Peterhof". The celebrated German poet Rainer Maria Rilke, to whom Benois showed the park from this point in 1900, exclaimed "It's the palace of the Snow Queen" and, so Benois recalled, tears of delight came to his eyes. Rilke recorded his impressions in the poem *On fountains*: "Suddenly I understood the essence of fountains, the mystery and phantom of glassy crowns."

**299**
Grand Cascade. Decorative sculpture:
*Wounded Amazon*. 1801, sculptor: Fedor Gordeev
Copy from an antique original dating from
the 5th–4th century B.C.

**300**
Grand Cascade. Decorative sculpture: *Ganymede*. 1800
Copy from an antique original by Leochares
Cast by Edmonde Gastecloux

## The Great Palace Interiors

The Great Palace is the main building of the Peterhof ensemble. Inside the Great Palace, the staterooms and drawing rooms are located on the first floor. Rastrelli made the largest of these the Throne Room, which has an area of 300 metres. A double row of windows in the Ballroom reflected in a series of mirrors visually increases the size of the hall. A large number of windows of different shapes and sizes interspersed with strategically placed mirrors were a common device used in Baroque

**301**
Great Palace. Main Staircase. 1750s, architect: Bartolomeo Rastrelli

**302**
Great Palace. Throne Room. 1763–1780

**303**
Great Palace. Ballroom

architecture to create the illusion of endless space and eliminate the boundary between the interior and the surrounding grounds.
The staterooms at Peterhof are characterised by a superabundance of paintings, one of the most notable of which is a portrait of Catherine the Great on horseback and dressed in the uniform of the Semenovsky Guards, which hangs on the east wall of the Throne Room. This is not one of the allegories that were so characteristic of the decorative painting of the Baroque, but an historical canvas showing the Empress on her way to Peterhof at the head of the Guards Regiment. The walls are also decorated with bas-reliefs of an allegorical nature by Ivan Prokofiev, namely *Truth and Virtue* and *Justice and Safety*, and on historical themes, such as *The Return of Sviatoslav* by Mikhail Kozlovsky and *The Baptism of Olga* by Andrei Ivanov. At the eastern end of the room is a special platform on which the throne stands.
Four pictures by Richard Paton depicting episodes from the naval battle at Chesma Bay hang on the opposite wall. Furthermore, around the edges of the room, in the spaces between the windows of the upper row, twelve oval portraits of members of the royal family are to be seen.
The palace's small Chinese Studies are unique works of art in their own right. Created to designs by Vallin de La Mothe, they are decorated with genuine Chinese lacquered screens brought to Russia during the time of Peterhof's first owner. The walls of the studies are upholstered with

crimson and gold silk. Against this rich background, the wooden panels of the screens painted with the miniature designs so characteristic of late 17th – early 18th century Chinese art are particularly striking. They show domestic scenes and landscapes as well as birds and animals, fruits and flowers. Chinese motifs were also used in the decoration of the varnished tiles with which the stoves in the respective studies are faced.

One of the oldest of the palace interiors is the Portrait Hall. In the Petrine era this was also the largest room. The big, two-tone hall in the very centre of the palace has windows and doors on two sides. To the south the Upper Park is to be seen, while to the north lie the Grand Cascade and the gulf in all their glory. Not only does this make the already impressive room with its 7 metre high walls all the more commanding, but more importantly, it establishes a link between the interior and the natural surroundings. The room's furnishings – the painted ceiling, illustrated medallions and gilded woodwork – do not detract from its principal treasures: the walls of the gallery are entirely covered with 368 portraits by the Italian artist Pietro Rotari. This kind of "wallpapering" was characteristic of palace interiors in the 18th century.

**304**
Great Palace
Western Chinese Study

**305**
Great Palace. Audience Chamber. 1750s,
architect: Bartolomeo Rastrelli

**306**
Great Palace. Blue Drawing Room. Banqueting service.
1848–1852. Imperial Porcelain Factory, St Petersburg

**307**
Great Palace. Portrait Hall. 1716–1724,
architects: Jean-Baptiste Leblond, Niccolo Michetti;
1764, architect: Jean-Baptiste Vallin de La Mothe

## The Lower Park Fountains

The Grand Cascade divides the Lower Park into east and west, each side having its own smaller cascade. In the eastern area of the park, the Chessboard Hill or Dragon Cascade adorns a natural incline. At its head, three fantastic winged dragons spit water from between their fanged jaws, which flows down a chequered slope. Both sides of the cascade are decorated with marble statues made by early 18th-century Italian masters. In front of the Chessboard Hill stand two Roman Fountains, which were created in the first half of the 18th century. They were originally made of wood, but were refashioned in marble at the end of the century. They resemble the two-tiered fountains on the square in front of St Peter's Cathedral in Rome. The ensemble of the Lower Park is distinguished by its unusual fountains, each of which is truly unique. Most of them are trick fountains intended for amusing visitors.
The Pyramid Fountain is completely different by design with its granite pedestal sat on three marble steps. This water obelisk is an impressive sight: seven tiers of foaming jets spring from over five hundred concealed apertures. Together with such monumental ornaments, the park

**308**
Pyramid Fountain. 1721–1724

**309**
Mushroom Fountain. 1735, sculptor: Carlo Rastrelli; engineer: Paul Sualem

**310**
Sun Fountain. 1724, architect: Niccolo Michetti
1772–1776, architects: Yuri Velten, I. Yakovlev

**311**
Eve Fountain. 1718, sculptor: Giovanni Bonazza
1725–1726, architect: Niccolo Michetti

**312**
Roman Fountain. 1738–1739; 1799–1800

also contains smaller, elegant fountains such as The Sun. The sound of the latter's murmuring streams is reminiscent of an intimate conversation, while the scattered sprays of its central jet lit up by varicoloured lights give the fountain its name.

Peterhof is famed largely for its fountains, which are both ingenious works of hydraulic engineering and masterpieces of monumental decorative art. The glittering, iridescent jets of the three cascades and the many fountains playing in the rays of the sun create the unique sensation of a celebration of nature and the apotheosis of Peter the Great's own favourite element – water. The variety of forms and the different functions played by the fountains make Peterhof an open-air museum unlike any other in the world. Each of the ornamental fountains in the grounds is the "hero" of a particular subject. The Adam and Eve fountains remind visitors that they are in a veritable earthly paradise. "The Favourite" is an illustration of La Fontaine's fable about a dog trying to catch ducks. The fountains desighed by Peter the Great himself can rival their most famous Peterhof counterparts.

**313**
View of the Seafront Terrace and the Monplaisir Palace

**314**
Orangery Fountain: *Triton Tearing Open the Jaws of a Sea Monster*
Early 18th century, sculptor: Antonio Tarsia

**315**
Monplaisir Garden. Bell Fountain
*Psyche*. 1817. Copy of the original by Antonio Canova

## Monplaisir

Peter I's favourite abode was the palace of Monplaisir, which is situated close to the sea and blends harmoniously with the coastal landscape. Adjoining the central part of this one-storey building crowned with a tall roof are two glass-walled galleries, which form a delightful promenade from which both the park and the sea can be viewed. The main room of this cosy little palace is the State Hall, which appears quite large due to its eight metre high ceiling. Splendid banquets and rowdy gatherings were often held here. "In Peter's day, Peterhof, or 'Peter's Court' as it was known then, teemed with life, and guests would feast here for several days at a time... There was also very little restraint at the table: at Peter Petrovich's christening, for example, a naked female dwarf appeared on the men's table from inside a huge cake, gave a speech to the guests and made a toast, while at the ladies table a naked

male dwarf did exactly the same thing. Everyone was drunk at the royal feasts regardless of whether they were male or female" (Mikhail Pyliaev). Today, the only reminder of these "assemblies" is the enormous Great Eagle Cup, which was passed to guests who were obliged, under strict surveillance and at great risk to their health, to drain it in one go.

**316**
Monplaisir. State Hall
**317**
Monplaisir. Side Gallery
**318**
Monplaisir Palace. 1714–1723, architects: Johann Braunstein, Jean-Baptiste Leblond, Niccolo Michetti, sculptor: Carlo Rastrelli
Designed by Peter I
Monplaisir Garden. 1714–1739, gardener: Leonard Garnichfeldt. Designed by Peter I
Wheatsheaf Fountain. 1721–1723, architect: Niccolo Michetti. Designed by Peter I
**319**
Ramp. Entrance to the Lower Park

### The Marly Palace and the Hermitage Pavilion

In the western part of the Lower Park, is the Marly ensemble the beauty and individuality of which win the hearts of all visitors to Peterhof. It was named in honour of its prototype, Marly le Rois, the residence of the French king, Louis XIV. The Peterhof Marly comprises three gardens (one of which is a water garden), the Golden Hill Cascade and, of course, several fountains. At the centre of the ensemble is the Marly Palace, standing between two ponds. The modest two-storey building is reflected in their mirror-like surfaces. The palace's indescribable beauty is most apparent on bright, calm days when the water of the ponds is still and the air is clear. The Marly Palace originally served as lodgings for distinguished persons, but later became a museum dedicated to the memory of its first owner. Here, many of Peter the Great's personal effects are to be seen along with genuine late 17th – early 18th-century artefacts. Inside the palace, on the ground and first floors, which are linked by an elegant staircase decorated with openwork, are eight small rooms.

On the ground floor is the Kitchen. Here, the walls and stove are covered with two-tone tiles, which are decorated with scenes of Dutch life. The main feature of the rooms, however, is a splendid collection of paintings by Dutch, Flemish and Italian masters of the 18th and 19th centuries. The view from the windows also lends the house an atmosphere all of its own. The Hermitage Pavilion (a title derived from the French for an anchorite's hut) is situated in the part of the Lower Park that is closest to the sea. The name indicates the purpose of such buildings, which were extremely popular in France in the 18th century and later in Russia.

**320**
Golden Hill Cascade. 1722–1725, architects: Niccolo Michetti, Johann Braunstein, Mikhail Zemtsov and T. Usov, sculptor: Carlo Rastrelli, engineer: Paul Sualem
Bell Fountain. 1732, architect: Mikhail Zemtsov

**321**
Panorama of the Lower Park around the Marly Palace

**322**
View of the Marly Palace, the semi-circular fishpond and the Garden of Venus from the Golden Hill Cascade

**323**
Golden Hill Cascade. South terrace

The Peterhof Hermitage was the first in Russia. The man behind its inception was, as always, Peter I, and in 1722 the building was erected in the Marly Garden. Its solitariness was further enhanced by a specially created moat spanned by a small bridge. Nothing was to disturb the intimate atmosphere of this house. On the first floor is the Upper Stateroom with an area of 80 square metres, where evening music recitals and intimate suppers were held. Its main feature was a special table with a system of hoists. It seated 14 people and was served from the Pantry on the ground floor. Special wooden pipes, through which plates could be passed, led to each setting at the table. A bell warned guests of the imminent appearance of their next dish.

**324**
Hermitage Pavilion. 1721–1757, architects: Johann Braunstein, Bartolomeo Rastrelli

**325**
An avenue in the Lower Park

**326**
Hermitage Pavilion. Upper Stateroom

**327**
Chessboard Hill (Dragon Cascade). 1737–1739, architects: Mikhail Zemtsov, Ivan Blank, I. Davydov; sculptor Hans Konrad Osner

**328**
Chessboard Hill (Dragon Cascade). Detail

## The Great Palace and the Upper Park

The architect Bartolomeo Rastrelli played a fundamental role in transforming the Upper Chambers, built back in the Petrine era, into the impressive formal edifice known today as the Great Palace. The latter swiftly became the compositional and artistic centrepiece of the Upper and Lower Parks. The interiors too were refurbished according to Rastrelli's designs, and both the use of space and the décor itself were in perfect accord with the purpose served by the palace. Although its appearance was shaped over the course of almost half a century, the basic threefold structure of the building was determined from the outset. In the mid-18th century, while preserving the basic design, Rastrelli enlarged the palace and thereby lent it a majestic air. The central three-storey component, of which only the middle section of the Petrine Upper Chambers remains, is linked by ground floor galleries to the two-storey side wings. To the west is the Coat of Arms Wing, so named because of the traditional emblem of the two-headed eagle perched atop the domed roof of the building. The coat of arms is 27 metres off the ground and a special device enables it to rotate like a weather vane. The figure of the eagle is ingeniously contrived: the presence of an extra head enables it to appear in all its double-headed glory no matter which way it turns. To the east, the architectural composition terminates in the Church, which is crowned with a central dome and a number of smaller gilded cupolas.

In front of the south wall of the Great Palace stretches the Upper Park. This plot of 15 hectares, divided into equal parts, is a marvellous example of regular landscape gardening. The main garden is framed with borders and hedges and encompasses four trelliswork summerhouses and four arbours. The fountains, however, play the most important part in the decorations of the garden, the most magnificent of which is the Neptune Fountain reflecting the popular theme of the sea. The centrepiece of this three-tiered fountain is the bearded bronze figure of Neptune, the ruler of the waves. In his hands he holds a trident, the typical attribute of his power, while on his head he wears a crown. At water level, statuesque horsemen seek to restrain plunging hippocampi surrounded by dolphins, dragons and Tritons, the escorts of the god of the sea.

**329**
Panoramic view of the Upper Park

**330**
Coat of Arms Wing. Detail of the cupola

**331**
View of the Coat of Arms Wing from the Neptune Fountain

**332**
Upper Park. Neptune Fountain. 1721–1724; 1799

## The Cottage Palace

At the beginning of the 19th century to the east of Petrine Peterhof an extensive landscaped park began to take shape, marked with its own distinctive architectural features. Of these, probably the most striking is the Cottage, built by Adam Menelaws for Nicholas I and his wife Alexandra Fedorovna, in whose honour the grounds came to be known as the Alexandria Park. English Gothic motifs with a highly romantic flavour were used to decorate the building both inside and out. English rural dwellings served as the prototype on which the Cottage is based: the heir apparent had been struck by the practicality and patriarchal comfort of such houses during a visit to England. Each of the rooms of the small, cosy palace boasts its own mural, which reflects the purpose of the chamber itself. All of these works, the most notable of which is the scene decorating the Staircase, were painted by the master of monumental decorative art, Giovanni Battista Scotti. Intricate stuccowork also plays an important part in the overall design of the interiors, lending them an extraordinary elegance and charm.
The Cottage houses a vast array of canvases, which adorn the walls of almost every single room.

A significant part of this collection is made up of thirty works (seascapes and scenes of coastal towns) by Ivan Aivazovsky, who was greatly admired by the imperial court.
The house was a particular favourite of the royal family. Here, the Empress ruled the roost. Alexandra Fedorovna's tastes were readily apparent in the décor of the rooms and the arrangement of the furniture: she personally selected the objects of applied art and paintings that were used to brighten the surroundings. Through her care and attention the Cottage became a genuine family home where the Emperor was able quite simply to be a loving husband and solicitous father. He even liked to refer to himself as the "Lord of the Cottage".

### The Sts Peter and Paul Cathedral

Work began on the construction of the Sts Peter and Paul Cathedral in Peterhof on 25 July 1895. The building was designed by the architect Sultanov, whose works incorporated unique embodiments of the traditions of Old Russian architecture. In his own words, "the motifs of the façade were inspired by the forms used in Russian churches of the 16th and 17th centuries, characterised by their particular richness and beauty." The murals and religious utensils were also created from designs and sketches by the architect himself. The building constitutes a unique many-tiered composition, crowned with five closely set cupolas and girded by a covered gallery for religious processions. Adjoined to the west wall are a three-flighted belfry, a chapel and two porches. The outer walls are covered with glazed bricks and tiles. Meanwhile, the interior of the church, with its three altars, was once stunningly beautiful and splendidly decorated. The main ornament of the central nave was a unique majolica iconostasis bearing icons on gilded bronze tablets and a silver crucifix. (This particular icon screen is currently being restored.) All of the iconostasis in the church were edged with white Carrara marble. Restoration began on the exterior of this fascinating monument to Neo-Russian architecture in 1975. In 1989, the church was handed over to the Petersburg Diocesan Department, which set about resurrecting it.

**333**
Alexandria Park. Cottage Palace. 1826–1842, architects: Adam Menelaws, Andrei Stackenschneider

**334**
Egor Botman. ? –1891. *Portrait of Nicholas I.* 1849

**335**
Cottage Palace. Empress' Drawing Room

**336**
Peterhof. Sts Peter and Paul Cathedral
1895–1904, architect: Nikolai Sultanov, assisted by Vasily Kosyakov

# Tsarskoye Selo

Tsarskoye Selo is associated primarily with the names of two Empresses, Elizabeth Petrovna and Catherine the Great. The initial development of the site began under Catherine I, Peter the Great's wife, who was given the land by the Emperor. However, it was only during the reign of her daughter, Elizabeth, and through the efforts of Francesco Bartolomeo Rastrelli, who believed that palaces should be created "for the common glory of Russia", that this residence could rightfully be called Tsarskoye Selo – the Tsar's Village.
In 1744, Elizabeth Petrovna commissioned Rastrelli to build "a palace with truly splendid ornaments, fit to be an abode for the ruler of a huge empire." "At first, while the palace was under construction, the ornaments gleamed, and when Empress Elizabeth arrived to view it in the company of her entire court and the foreign ministers, they were all stunned by its splendour, and each of the courtiers rushed to express his amazement" (Mikhail Pyliaev).
Besides its importance as a royal residence, Tsarskoye Selo is also linked to certain prominent Russian cultural figures and events. Even before the days of the great Alexander Pushkin who was schooled there, Tsarskoye Selo was the site of an incident that was to be of great significance in the development of national theatre. A group of actors, under the direction of the son of the Yaroslavl merchant Fedor Volkov, made its first

**337**
Catherine Palace. Cupolas of the palace church
**338**
Catherine Palace. Central part of the façade seen from the garden
**339**
Detail of the palace exterior

appearance before a royal audience in the Catherine Palace. Empress Elizabeth, who had heard a great deal about the talents of the young actors, wished to witness them for herself. Delighted by what she saw, Elizabeth invited Volkov and his associates to Petersburg, and in 1756 she issued a decree on the founding of the Russian professional theatre. Besides staterooms, drawing rooms and living quarters, Rastrelli incorporated a chapel into his designs for the palace. It became known as the Church of the Resurrection and stood in the east wing of the building. The foundations of the chapel were laid with great pomp and circumstance in the presence of the Royal family.

**340**
View of the Catherine Palace from the park

**341**
Evgueny Lanceray. 1875–1946
*Empress Elizabeth Petrovna at Tsarskoye Selo.* 1905

**342**
Catherine Palace. 1752–1756,
architect: Bartolomeo Rastrelli; sculptor: Johann Dunker

## The Catherine Palace

Rastrelli remodelled the main features of the park and palace ensemble for Elizabeth Petrovna, although they are historically known as the Catherine Park and Catherine Palace respectively. The architect not only completely altered the dimensions of the latter, but also adorned them with lavish sculptural designs inside and out. The palace's external ornaments give a highly accurate impression of the creativeness and imagination of the architect, who succeeded in endowing the 300 metre long façade with a plastic expressiveness. No expense was spared on this building: approximately 100 kilos of gold alone were used in the decorations. Rastrelli perfected the regular park that had been planned earlier, stretching out to the north of the Catherine Palace, and completed the construction of a number of park pavilions. One of these was the Hermitage, intended for the Empress's amusement and solitary leisure. Rastrelli's work as an interior designer can best be judged by the décor of the Grand Hall. This enormous room with an area of 846 square metres is permeated with a sense of greatness and majesty. Bright and airy, it seems even larger than it actually is because of the many mirrors, the abundance of gilding and, in particular, the spectacular painted ceiling, which creates an illusion of endless space. Rastrelli wanted the room to be perceived as an integral whole, so he concealed the stoves necessary to heat this huge hall behind false windows with mirrored glass.

**343**
Catherine Palace. Grand Hall. Detail of the interior
**344**
Catherine Palace. Grand Hall. 1752–1756, architect: Bartolomeo Rastrelli
**345**
Louis Tocque. 1696–1772. *Portrait of Empress Elizabeth Petrovna*

The famous Main Staircase fashioned in marble by Ippolit Monighetti, is striking for the monumental character of its design.
During Catherine II's reign, new interiors appeared in the palace, connected to the name of Charles Cameron. The use of subtly adapted forms derived from Greco-Roman décor is characteristic of the works of this outstanding master of Classicism. This is particularly apparent in the design of the Bedchamber, the largest of Paul I and Maria Fedorovna's private rooms. Elegant alcoves and refined decorations lend the chamber a special charm. The slender faience columns entwined with garlands and arranged with a subtle sense of rhythm, the stucco frieze (sculptor: Ivan Martos) against the pale green walls, and the delicately gilded mouldings are all reminiscent of the features

**346**
Catherine Palace. Bedchamber
**347**
Catherine Palace. Bedchamber. Detail of the doors
**348**
Catherine Palace. Blue Drawing Room
**349**
Catherine Palace. Main Staircase
1860, architect: Ippolit Monighetti

of the famous Pompeiian villas. Cameron especially loved to use unusual combinations of painting, gilding, decorative fabrics and items of furniture in his interiors. In the Blue Drawing Room, for example, pale blue silk with a flower print serves as a delightful backdrop for the austere Classical forms of the furniture and mirrors. The standard lamps made of blue glass and positioned in the corners of the room make a delightful addition to its decorative fittings. This room is the most elegant of all the interiors designed by Cameron. Next door is the Chinese Blue Drawing Room, otherwise known as the Main Study. The silks and porcelain fittings used in the décor of this chamber were brought to Russia in the mid-18th century when trade links with China began to develop. In Charles Cameron's day, fireplaces for heating the vast rooms first appeared in the palace chambers and were constructed precisely according to his designs.
The Picture Hall, next-door to the Amber Room, still looks the way Rastrelli first designed it.

**350**
Catherine Palace. Main Staircase. Upper landing

**351**
Catherine Palace. Chinese Blue Drawing Room. Detail

**352**
Catherine Palace. Green Dining Room

**353**
Catherine Palace. Chinese Blue Drawing Room

This two-tone room spans the entire width of the palace, with windows facing both east and west. It was created to house a collection of 17th – early 18th-century European paintings, which was purchased abroad in 1745.
One of the main features of the palace at Tsarskoye Selo was, without a doubt, the famous Amber Room. In 1717, small amber boards and four amber panels were sent as a gift to Peter the Great by the Prussian king, Frederick I. Anyone who ever saw the Amber Room was enchanted by it. One French author once wrote that: "The eye, unused to seeing amber in such quantities, is captivated and blinded by the wealth and warmth of the tones, which encompass every shade of yellow, from dusky topaz to bright lemon…" During the war, the Amber Room was looted. The current exhibition is comprised of the works that were saved or restored. The amber mosaics lining the walls are being recreated by contemporary craftsmen. Hopefully, the room will regain its former splendour in the very near future.

**354**
Catherine Palace. Amber Room. Detail of the interior
**355**
Catherine Palace. Amber Room
**356**
Catherine Palace. Picture Hall

**357**
Façade of the Catherine Palace seen from the pond
**358**
Cameron Gallery. View of the colonnade
**359**
Cameron Gallery. 1784–1787, architect: Charles Cameron
**360**
Cameron Gallery. Main Staircase
**361**
View of the Agate Rooms from the Hanging Garden

## The Catherine Park

In 1728, Tsarskoye Selo became the property of Elizabeth Petrovna following an edict issued by Peter I. Before ascending to the throne, she often came here to hunt and oversee the cultivation of the orchards on the estate. Rastrelli perfected the regular park that had been planned earlier, stretching out to the north of the Catherine Palace, and completed the construction of a number of park pavilions. One of these was the Hermitage, intended for the Empress's amusement and solitary leisure. The oldest part of the Catherine Park is the Upper Garden, which stretches out before the north façade of the Catherine Palace. Its avenues are lined with marble sculptures. Only a small number of the statues and busts that were to be found here in the 18th and 19th centuries have survived to this day. Several of them bear inscriptions. The names of masters of the Venetian school at the turn of the 18th century – Pietro Baratta, Antonio Tarsia and Giovanni Bonazza – are to be seen on the pedestals. Works by these sculptors also grace the Summer Garden in Petersburg. It was Baratta who created one of the best statues in the Upper Garden, the representation of Galatea. This small statue was conceived as the centrepiece of a fountain. Although it is difficult to imagine the regular park devoid of fountains, it indeed had none due to the lack of water sources from which to power them. This was not surprising: there was even a shortage of drinking water in Tsarskoye Selo and the imperial court had to bring a supply with it whenever it visited the summer residence.

The Empress Catherine II devoted much time and care to the development of the estate and "here her genius and fine taste were revealed". "Travelling to Tsarskoye with a small retinue, Catherine divided her time between affairs of state and all manner of amusements. Every day she would take a walk in the park in the company of the knights and maids of the court... Of all the country residences, Catherine's favourite was Tsarskoye Selo. From 1763 onwards, with the exception of 2–3 years, she lived in Tsarskoye Selo in spring and spent practically all summer here, leaving in the autumn when the weather grew cold. It is here that she celebrated almost every one of her birthdays, and from here that she set out on her ceremonial journey to Petersburg on 28 June 1763 after the coronation in Moscow" (Serguei Vilchkovsky). Under Catherine II, the vast park with an area of 100.5 hectares became a "pantheon of Russian greatness". The unique ensemble of monuments, which includes the Chesma Column and the Column

**362**
Cameron Ramp. 1792–1794, architect Charles Cameron

**363**
View of the Cameron Gallery from one of the arches of the ramp

of Morea, the Kagul Obelisk and the Crimean Column, commemorates the Turkish campaigns of the 1770s and 80s, the crowning glory of the Russian forces.
Around the same time, buildings that now constitute stylish monuments to Russian Classicism were also erected in the Catherine Park. Catherine II once described the work of Cameron in one of her letters: "Now I have got my hands on the master Cameron, a Scotsman by birth, a Jacobin by profession and a great draughtsman, who is full of knowledge of the ancients and is renowned for his book on ancient bathhouses. Here in Tsarskoye Selo we are creating a terraced garden with bathhouses below and a gallery above. It will be charming!" It was not the interiors that brought Charles Cameron the fame he deserved, but the splendid architectural edifices that he built, of which there are several in Tsarskoye Selo. The largest and most illustrious of these is the Cameron Gallery, named after its designer.
The Gallery and the adjoining Agate Rooms, Cold Bath, Hanging Gardens and Ramp make up a harmonious "Greco-Roman rhapsody". Indeed, this architectural composition, which comprises several buildings created to serve a variety of functions, is inspiring for its grandeur, originality and the boldness of its design.
The Cameron Gallery, intended for meditation, promenades, social intercourse and contemplation of the splendid landscape that stretches out on all sides, plays an important part in the ensemble. The architect chose a truly appropriate spot for it on the slope of the hill leading down to the Great Pond. The ground floor of the Gallery is made of massive stone blocks. Here were the living quarters for courtiers. The bright, glass-faced hall on the first floor, surrounded on all sides by a colonnade, seems still lighter and airier in comparison to the solid ground floor.
The magnificent outer staircase with its elegantly curving flight of steps is a wonderful architectural creation in its own right.
The Gallery is decorated with busts of philosophers, poets, Emperors, military leaders, gods and heroes of antiquity. The only contemporary of Cameron's whose likeness is included in this series is Mikhail Lomonosov.
The two-storey building of the Agate Rooms is angled towards the sun just as Roman thermal baths were. On the lower floor are the Cold Baths for which Cameron devised

**364, 366, 367**
Catherine Park. Decorative sculptures
17th–18th century
**365**
Catherine Park. Terrace

a special plumbing system. The second floor is occupied by the Agate Rooms themselves, named after the material with which the walls, columns and pilasters are covered (they are also faced with jasper). The interiors of all the rooms are amazing for the harmonious combination of architecture, painting and sculpture.
The Ramp installed by Cameron serves as an organic link between the architectural ensemble and the surrounding landscaped gardens.
It also represents one of Cameron's artistic triumphs. The décor of the walls is eye-catching: enormous masks cut from local limestone adorn the keystones of the arches. Amongst the heroes of ancient mythology to be seen here are Mercury, Pan, Silenus, Neptune and others. The Ramp is also decorated with wrought iron tripods, attributed to Vasily Stasov.
Besides the palace and the Cameron Gallery, the Catherine Park contains a number of small pavilions, which serve various purposes. Often located on the shores of a pond or lake, they are magically reflected in the still surface of the waters. The Grotto or Morning Room blends beautifully with the panorama of the Great Pond. It is a characteristic example of the small architectural structures that adorn the horizons of the park at Tsarskoye Selo. From the 1770s onwards, a preoccupation with "historical" styles such as the Gothic and, in particular, the Oriental "Turkic" and "Chinoiserie" styles, became apparent in the

architecture within the gardens. On the shore of the Great Pond, for example, the Admiralty ensemble, consisting of three buildings, was created. The name is derived from the fact that the central structure was used as a boat-house. Its round turret and the arrow slits cut into the brick walls are a testimony to the English Gothic style.
In the Catherine Park, on the southwest shore of the Great Pond, stands the Turkish Bath. Built in honour of Russia's victory over the Turks in the war of 1828–1829, its design embodies a Turkish theme. Having given his brainchild the external appearance of a mosque

**368**
Catherine Park. Chesma Column
1774–1776, architect: Antonio Rinaldi

**369**
View of the bridges near the Concert Hall

**370**
Catherine Park. Admiralty ("Holland")
Aviary. 1773–1777, architect: Vasily Neyelov

**371**
Cameron Gallery. Decorative vase

**372**
Catherine Park. Turkish Bath
1850–1852, architect: Ippolit Monighetti

with three-tiered minarets, the architect then embellished the interior with genuine articles of Eastern applied art, namely marble slabs taken from fountains and carved with verses in Arabic.
In the 1770s, the architect Neyelov erected a remarkable bridge over the Great Pond. It was initially referred to as the Siberian Marble Gallery, since its component parts were prepared in Ekaterinburg from marble mined in the Urals and delivered to Tsarskoye Selo, where they were assembled over a period of two years. It subsequently came to be known as the Palladian Bridge in honour of the famous Italian architect and theoretician, Andrea Palladio.

**373**
Catherine Park
Grotto (Morning Room). 1749–1761, architect: Bartolomeo Rastrelli

**374**
Catherine Park. Palladian Bridge
1772–1774, architect: Vasily Neyelov

**375**
Catherine Park
Fountain: *The Milkmaid, or the Girl with a Pitcher*
1816, sculptor: Pavel Sokolov

## The Chinese Village

The Chinoiserie style found its embodiment at Tsarskoye Selo in a number of bridges in the Catherine Park and, in particular, in the ensemble known as the Chinese Village. The latter comprises 10 houses with intricate lines and decorative curved roofs. Situated in the Alexander Park, this complex is linked to the Catherine Park by two bridges. One of these is the Great Caprice, which constitutes a unique work of park architecture. The bridge is crowned with an elegant pagoda in which the European form of the octagonal rotunda is combined with an Eastern-style upturned roof. The second is the Cross Bridge, a fascinating structure consisting of two intersecting spans. On the bridge itself stands an octagonal pavilion with a curved roof, which sports an ornamental spike topped with a sphere.

**376, 378**
Alexander Park
Chinese Village. 1782–1798, architects: Vasily Neyelov, Charles Cameron, Antonio Rinaldi; 1817–1822, architect: Vasily Stasov

**377**
Alexander Park. Cross Bridge
1776–1779, architect: Vasily Neyelov

**379**
Alexander Park. Great Caprice. 1770s–1780s, architects: Vasily Neyelov, Giacomo Quarenghi

**The Lyceum**

Tsarskoye Selo is not simply dear to Russians because it was one of the imperial country residences for many years. This place is also inseparably linked to the name of the great Russian poet Alexander Pushkin, who studied at the Lyceum (now a branch of the Pushkin Museum) and continued to visit the village at various times throughout his life. Even people who have not been to Tsarskoye Selo can clearly picture its various features and get a feel for their charms when reading the poet's verses. It seems that the writer extols every inch of the park, including the renowned "Milkmaid Fountain" (1816, sculptor: Pavel Sokolov), which was built over the only natural spring in the park. Not far from the fountain is a statue depicting a youthful Pushkin in the gardens of Tsarskoye Selo.
On 8 January 1815 in the Assembly Hall of the Lyceum, one of the most important events in the life of Pushkin and the history of Russian poetry took place. Eminent guests, including the outstanding 18th-century Russian poet Gavriil Derzhavin, were invited to attend the examinations at the Lyceum, during which the young Pushkin read a poem that he had composed specially for the occasion, entitled "Recollections of Tsarskoye Selo". Many years later the poet wrote: "I only saw Derzhavin once, but I will never forget it... He dozed right up until the Russian literature examination,

at which point he was completely transformed… At last, my name was called… I cannot describe the state I was in: when I got to the part where I refer to Derzhavin, my voice turned into an adolescent squeak and my heart began to pound with intoxicating delight… I do not recall how I finished the recital; I do not remember where I ran off to. Derzhavin was enraptured, he wanted to embrace me. They looked for me, but they could not find me." That is how Pushkin won his first poetic acclaim. He was fifteen years old.

**380**
Cupola of the Catherine Palace Chapel

**381**
Statue of Pushkin in the garden of the Lyceum. 1900, sculptor: Robert Bach

**382**
View of the Catherine Palace Chapel and the Lyceum

**383**
Ilya Repin. 1844–1930. *Pushkin at the Lyceum Examination in Tsarskoye Selo on 8 January 1815.* 1911

## The Alexander Palace

In the mid-18th century, the main entrance to the palace was located on the south side of the building. A large courtyard was laid out before it, surrounded by a decorative fence with gilded details. The gateway was crowned with the Russian coat of arms.
Beyond the bounds of the main estate at Tsarskoye Selo lies another famous park. The Alexander Park was laid in the early 19th century and combines regular gardens and landscaped features.
The architectural and aesthetic centrepiece of the park is the Alexander Palace, a delightful building designed by Giacomo Quarenghi. The palace's façades are very simple. They are adorned with colonnades comprising double rows of Corinthian columns. The design of the palace blends subtly with the surrounding landscape so that the building becomes an integral part of the natural setting rather than the dominant feature.

**384**
Egyptian Gate. 1827–1830, architects: Adam Menelaws, I. Ivanov
**385**
Alexander Palace. 1792–1796, architect: Giacomo Quarenghi
**386**
Alexander Palace. Nicholas II's New Study
**387**
Vladimir Makovsky. 1846–1920
*Portrait of Nicholas II*

Catherine II commissioned the building of this palace for her favourite grandson, Alexander I. She personally oversaw the education of Paul's eldest son, and patronised him in a number of ways. The Empress wanted to make him her heir in order to deprive Paul, whom she disliked, of his right to the throne and thus vex her son even from beyond the grave.
When Alexander I became Emperor after the assassination of his father, which was committed with Alexander's mute consent, the palace was given to the future tsar, Grand Duke Nicholas. Alexander III also lived there prior to his ascension to the throne, and Nicholas II chose the palace as his permanent residence. The Alexander Palace became the last refuge of the royal family after Nicholas II was deposed in 1917. From here, he and his family were taken to Tobolsk and then to Ekaterinburg, where they were executed in July 1918.
The palace interiors suffered during the war. In the summer of 1997, a permanent exhibition was opened in the left wing of the building. Today, certain elements of the Reception Room, Nicholas II's New Study and Alexandra Fedorovna's Corner Drawing Room have been recreated and provide a fascinating backdrop to the exhibitions of historical costumes, weapons and objects of applied art to be found within their walls. In Nicholas II's beautifully preserved Study, where the working environment of the last Russian Emperor has been recreated, hangs a portrait of Nicholas II's father painted by the great Russian artist, Valentin Serov. In the children's quarters, visitors can see dresses once worn by the grand princesses and outfits and toys belonging to the tsarevich, Alexei.

## The Egyptian Gates

The architectural wonders of Tsarskoye Selo are not only to be seen in the grounds of the parks, but also in the town. On the road that runs alongside the Alexander Park, the Egyptian Gates, designed by Menelaws, were erected in 1827–1830. The gateposts that flank the arch resemble truncated pyramids. They are decorated with rows of reliefs showing genuine Egyptian characters. The stylised stems of the sacred Egyptian flower, the lotus, are entwined in the metal grille. These gates formed the main entrance to the town from the Petersburg side.

**388**
View of the gates and main courtyard of the Catherine Palace

**389**
Main gates. Detail

# Pavlovsk

The park and palace ensemble of Pavlovsk is situated just south of Tsarskoye Selo. In 1777, Catherine II made a gift of the extensive hunting grounds along the banks of the Slavianka River to her son Paul, and two years later work began on the construction of a formal palace and the landscaping of the natural environs. Created within a relatively short space of time (from the late 1770s to the early 1800s), it became the only country estate on the outskirts of Petersburg to have complete stylistic integrity. Within just twenty years of the laying of the first foundations, the Pavlovsk ensemble was already an inspiration to those who saw it.
Two generations of Classical architects, renowned for their professional contributions to the city of Petersburg, worked at Pavlovsk.
The first and most important Pavlovsk architect was Charles Cameron, whose name is primarily associated in the history of Russian architecture with the buildings he designed for this estate.
The palace built for the crown prince, Paul, and his family became the dominant architectural feature at Pavlovsk. By design the palace is a threefold structure, consisting of a central section in which the staterooms and living quarters are located, and two side wings for the servants, which, together with the semicircular galleries that join them, delineate the main courtyard.
The unusually elegant gold and white façade of the central section of the palace was built to designs by Charles Cameron between 1782 and 1785. It looks particularly striking from the banks of the Slavianka, which flows at the foot of the hill on which this delightful edifice stands.
The crown prince, Paul Petrovich, and his wife, Maria Fedorovna, put a great deal of effort into turning their family nest into one of Europe's most beautiful palaces. Within the walls of their residence they assembled an extensive collection of paintings, porcelain, ornamental metalwork and furniture. Under the names of Count and Countess Severny (meaning literally, Northern), the royal couple travelled around the continent familiarising themselves with the latest trends in European art and purchasing a great number of works. Paul and Maria Fedorovna's impeccable artistic tastes enabled

**390**
Statue of Paul I in front of Pavlovsk Palace. 1872
Copy from an original by Ivan Vitali

**391**
View of Pavlovsk Palace
from one of the northern pavilions

**392**
Panorama of Pavlovsk Palace

them to identify the finest embodiments of the new Classical trends of the day. After the murder of Emperor Paul I, his widow became the sole owner of the palace and parks at Pavlovsk, and nurturing its aesthetic development became her overriding preoccupation. Sophie Dorothea of Württemberg, the future Maria Fedorovna, came to Russia from a small German town when she was 16 years of age. She made a significant contribution to the cultural evolution of her new homeland. Famous writers and poets of the times gathered at the salon of the widowed Empress, causing Pavlovsk to become known as the "Russian Parnassus". Maria Fedorovna compiled the first catalogue of the collections of artworks at Pavlovsk with a description of each of the objects on view there. As an enthusiastic housewife, Maria Fedorovna was also extremely keen on gardening and oversaw the development of the parks of Pavlovsk with great interest.

## The Pavlovsk Palace Interiors

It is not only the wonderful architecture – one of the crowning glories of the epoch of Russian Classicism – and the splendid ornamental fittings of its interiors that have brought Pavlovsk Palace the world-wide acclaim it deserves. The valuable canvases and antique sculptures together with the magnificent array of Russian and French furniture, tapestries, bronzes, assorted clocks, ornamental vases and chandeliers to be found in the palace make it a prominent historical and artistic landmark in Russian culture.
It is to Charles Cameron that the Lower or Egyptian Vestibule owes its striking appearance, so named because of the twelve Ancient Egyptian-style statues that line the walls. Above their heads medallions depicting the signs of the zodiac are to be seen, while at their feet lie the attributes of the months, symbolising man's various seasonal pursuits. These sculptures (1803–1804) were created from sketches by Andrei Voronikhin, who was invited to work on the restoration of the palace interiors after the building was damaged by fire in 1803.
From the Lower Vestibule one ascends a sweeping staircase to the first floor where the Upper or Main Vestibule is located, furnished in 1789 to designs by Vincenzo Brenna. From this room a decorative wooden door, created from sketches by Giacomo Quarenghi, opens onto the Italian Hall, which lies in the centre of the palace. This is one of the most glorious of the staterooms. The interior design is the work of Cameron, who derived his inspiration from antique architecture. The hall is crowned with a high dome with skylights all round, reminiscent of a Roman rotunda. The walls of the room are punctuated with curved niches housing genuine works of Roman sculpture, themselves copies of Greek originals.
The piers of the niches are decorated with antique reliefs. The arches of the hall's upper gallery repeat the curves of the niches at ground level, creating a sensation of buoyancy and pellucidness. Light plays an important part in the aesthetic image of this particular room.

**393**
Pavlovsk Palace. Grecian Hall

**394**
Pavlovsk Palace. Egyptian Vestibule

**395**
Pavlovsk Palace
Great Throne Room (State Dining Room)

**396**
Pavlovsk Palace. Great Throne Room
Girandole. Late 18th century
Imperial Glass Works, St Petersburg

**397**
Pavlovsk Palace. Third Anteroom
Clock. Late 18th century
Workshop of Pierre-Auguste Caron

During the daytime, the natural light that gently filters down from above creates an atmosphere of intimacy and mystery. At night, when the incredibly beautiful chandeliers and French horn-shaped candelabras are lit, the room becomes truly majestic and commanding. The Italian Hall was originally designed by Vincenzo Brenna, and later, after the fire of 1803, it was redeveloped by the architect Voronikhin.
In 1789, Brenna created another magnificent room in the Pavlovsk Palace, the Grecian Hall. This room too was restored by Voronikhin following the fire of 1803. The room is lined with a Corinthian colonnade, which gives it the appearance of a Greek peristyle. The Roman-style marble lamps situated between the columns are also reminiscent of antiquity.
The stuccowork on the ceiling, the depictions of Roman armour and weapons on the walls and the plaster copies of antique statues in the niches lend this room a particularly lavish and august air. Voronikhin incorporated two unique white marble fireplaces into the interior of the Grecian Hall, which had been made to sketches by Brenna for the Mikhailovsky Castle.
The furniture of the Pavlovsk Palace was created from drawings by Voronikhin. During the era of Classicism in the early 19th century it was common for architects to design items of applied art as well as the buildings that housed them. In the southern part of the palace lies the State Bedroom (1792, architect: Vincenzo Brenna), which was no less luxurious than any of the bedchambers to be found in the royal residences of France. The walls of the room are covered with silk panels painted with tempera. They are generously laden with depictions of fruit, musical instruments and agricultural

**398**
Pavlovsk Palace. Italian Hall
**399**
View of the east façade of Pavlovsk Palace
**400**
Alexander Roslin. 1718–1793
*Portrait of Maria Fedorovna.* 1777

implements – symbols of "rustic joy". The ceiling of the bedchamber is designed to resemble the trellis of a bower entwined with vines. Through the gaps in the greenery glimpses of peacocks can be seen, representing domestic happiness. The State Bedroom also contains a unique suite of furniture, the work of Henri Jacob, together with the toilette presented to Paul Petrovich and his wife by Marie Antoinette. The cobalt blue porcelain of each of the 64 items of the toilet set is decorated with delicate gold designs, while two cups bear the portraits of Marie Antoinette and Louis XVI. The palace's Picture Gallery occupies a room that forms a sweeping curve and is lined on both sides with windows, filling the room with natural light (1798, architect: Vincenzo Brenna). The pictures are hung according to a strict decorative principle. Amongst the many European paintings the most eye-catching are the works of the Flemish masters. The collection also includes canvases painted by celebrated European artists at the request of the palace's owners. The Great Throne Room situated in the south wing of the palace is the work of the architect Brenna. It is here that Paul I received the knights of the Order of Malta. The vast room (400 sq. m.) was originally rather low-ceilinged: the architect was reluctant to make

**401**
Pavlovsk Palace. Picture Gallery

**402**
Pavlovsk Palace. State Bedroom

**403**
Pavlovsk Palace. Lantern Study

it any larger for fear of detracting from the main suites in the central section of the palace. A brilliant master of perspective painting, Pietro Gonzago, proposed three designs for ceiling paintings that would visually increase the height of the room and create an illusion of spaciousness. It was only upon the restoration of the palace in 1957 that one of Gonzago's ideas was realised by a group of artists working under the direction of Anatoly Treskin. Today, the imperial tableware is on display in the Great Throne Room, including the famous Gold Dinner Service comprised of over 600 pieces (1828, Imperial Porcelain Factory, St Petersburg). More modest but no less beautiful and elegant apartments are located on the ground floor of the palace. One of the finest examples of these is the Lantern Study (1807, architect: Andrei Voronikhin). The latter is regarded as a peerless masterpiece of early 19th-century Russian interior design. The architect substituted the outer wall of the room with a semicircular oriel window overlooking the Private Garden, thereby creating a link between the palace interior and the surrounding landscape.

**404–407**
Pavlovsk Palace
Exhibition of 19th – early 20th century interiors

## Pavlovsk Park

In 1794, one foreign visitor to Pavlovsk made the following observations: "The garden is huge and laid out in the English style with hedges, meandering paths, the Slavianka, waterfalls, ponds, summerhouses, small buildings and several monuments."
The original idea and the general concept behind the layout of the main areas of the park, which now covers an area of 600 hectares, were conceived by Charles Cameron. Work began in 1782 with the laying of the main pathways leading from the palace, around which a stretch of regular park was created. Over ten pavilions were erected during the first stage of the creation of the ensemble designed by Cameron, which subsequently became the compositional centrepieces of various corners of the park. The most notable of these is the Temple of Friendship (1780–1782), the architect's first work in Russia. He built the rotunda on a small peninsula and encircled it with a ring of 16 columns. The Temple of Friendship, which presents a gorgeous sight from a variety

**408**
Pavlovsk Park. Centaur Bridge. 1799–1805, architects: Charles Cameron, Andrei Voronikhin

**409**
Pavlovsk Park. Old Sylvia. Statue: *Apollo of Belvedere*. 1798. Copy of an antique original
Cast by Edmonde Gastecloux

of viewpoints, is a wonderful complement to the romantic beauty of the landscape. Cameron's last architectural contribution to Pavlovsk was the Pavilion of the Three Graces (1800–1801), a portico in the guise of an ancient temple. Its pediments are decorated with high reliefs depicting the gods Apollo and Minerva (sculptor: Ivan Prokofiev). The edifice was given its current title in 1803 when a sculptural group by Paolo Triscorni showing three female figures supporting a vase was installed inside. Cameron envisaged Pavlovsk Park as the abode of the god and patron of the arts, Apollo, and the refuge of the Muses. The architect erected the so-called Apollo Colonnade (1782–1783) almost at the entrance to the park from the Tsarskoye Selo side, a horseshoe-shaped structure somewhat akin to a Classical rotunda with a double row of sturdy columns crowned by the vault of the heavens. The material chosen for this work was grey limestone, the coarseness of which was intended to give the impression that the monument dated from a bygone era.
In the centre of the colonnade stands a statue of Apollo Belvedere (1782, cast from a mould of the antique original).
After Cameron's dismissal, Vincenzo Brenna assumed responsibility for the further development of the park. In particular, he busied himself with designs for the layout of two new areas, which came to be known as Old and New Sylvia respectively (from the Latin for "forest"). Old Sylvia is a quiet, secluded part of the park at the centre of which is a small circular clearing with twelve avenues leading from it. It is decorated with a bronze sculpture, the subject of which perpetuated Cameron's notion of Pavlovsk as the abode of Apollo. The sculpture of the god (1782, cast from a wax model by Fedor Gordeev) stands in the centre of the clearing in the New Sylvia surrounded by figures of the nine Muses, Venus, Flora and Mercury (1782, cast from wax models by Fedor Gordeev), which are placed between the pathways. These sculptures blend in beautifully with the landscape, lending the ensemble a special charm.

**410**
Pavlovsk Park. Statue: *Erminia.* Mid-19th century, sculptor: Rinaldo Rinaldi

**411**
Pavlovsk Park. Apollo Colonnade
1782–1783, architect: Charles Cameron

**412**
Pavlovsk Park. Monumental staircase
Descent to the Slavianka valley

**413**
Pavlovsk Palace. 1782–1786, architect: Charles Cameron; 1786–1799, architect: Vincenzo Brenna; 1800–1825, architects: Giacomo Quarenghi, Andrei Voronikhin, Carlo Rossi

A large part in the design of the park was played by Pietro di Gottardo Gonzago, who also contributed to the palace interiors. He created entire landscaped areas that highlighted the inherent beauty of the natural surroundings themselves. As an architect and set designer, Gonzago devised a special system for planting trees and shrubs based on the different times at which they bloomed and faded to ensure that the park would be a riot of colour from early spring to late autumn, in other words the entire time that the members of the royal family would be inhabiting the summer residence.
Pavlovsk Park is characterised by the highly original and diverse artistic trends in park and garden design that prevail within its confines. The landscaped areas that expose nature's charms, together with the many pavilions, architectural structures and sculptures have brought great repute to the Pavlovsk ensemble.
The park is not only adorned with Classical monuments, however. Amidst the thickets of trees and shrubs on the banks of the river, occasional glimpses of structures of a completely different kind may be caught. In accord with the wishes of his employers, who paid tribute to the sentimental, romantic moods that were fashionable at the time, Charles Cameron built the Dairy (1782), a "theatrical" rendering of a settler's abode. It is hidden in the thick of the woods not far from the palace. Made of rough stones and thatched with straw, the outer shell of the Dairy does not betray any of the elegance and luxury hidden inside. Here, the members of the ruling elite and their guests would rest during their walks in the park and drink fresh milk from the cows that were pastured nearby. One of Vincenzo Brenna's buildings was the Peel Tower (1795–1797) with a water mill in the spirit of the senti-

mental, idyllic conceits of the 18th century. It was an imitation of an old ruin adapted for living purposes by settlers. However, as with the Dairy, the cosy and beautifully finished interior was a far cry from the building's modest exterior.
The Pavlovsk architectural and park ensemble is an outstanding monument to early 19th-century Russian culture. The beauty of Pavlovsk Park and the expressive designs of the palace and pavilions alike have always held a great attraction for artists.

**414**
Pavlovsk Park. Pavilion of the Three Graces
1800–1801, architect: Charles Cameron

**415**
Pavlovsk Park. Peel Tower
1795–1797, architect: Vincenzo Brenna,
designed by Pietro Gonzago

**416**
Temple of Friendship. 1780–1782, architect: Charles Cameron; 1799, architect: Vincenzo Brenna (reconstruction)

**417**
Monument to Maria Fedorovna. 1914, sculptor:
Vladimir Beklemishev

# Gatchina

The name Gatchina by which both the town and imperial estate located there are known dates back a long way and is probably derived from either the Russian expression *gat' chinit'* ("mend the road"), or, as others would have you believe, the Germanic *hat schone* ("has beauty"). The earliest reference to Gatchina is to be found in a ledger dating from 1499, in which certain lands adjoining the Muscovite state were listed.
The territory of Gatchina, which for many years previously had belonged to the principality of Novgorod, was under Swedish dominion in the 17th century. It was reclaimed from the Swedes during the Northern War, and in 1702 became a part of the Russian state. Peter I bestowed the land upon his favourite sister, Natalia. After her death, it became the property of various private owners. In 1765, Catherine II presented Gatchina to her famous favourite, Grigory Orlov, as a sign of her gratitude for the part he had played in placing her on the throne. That moment marked the beginning of the rich history of a magnificent country estate, which was spectacular even in Orlov's day.
Antonio Rinaldi, who had come to Russia in 1751 and become architect to the crown prince, was appointed to build a palace, the foundations of which were laid on 30 May 1766. The building, reminiscent of a medieval castle, was an imposing colossus with twin square towers. Curved wings linked the main section to a pair of symmetrically placed outbuildings.

**418**
Gatchina Palace. 1766–1781, architect: Antonio Rinaldi

**419**
Salvatore Tonci. 1756–1844. *Portrait of Paul I*

## Gatchina Palace

This castle-like construction stands on the crest of a row of hills. Its north façade overlooks a stretch of green land, which opens out at the foot of the rise and borders a lake. The south façade opens out onto a parade ground on which the changing of the guards and military demonstrations were once held. Along the outer edge of the square runs a low parapet complete with embrasures for weapons.
The castle-like image is completed by a moat. The silhouette of the palace is clean and sharp, accented by a pair of pentagonal, five-tiered towers, known as the Watchtower and the Signal Tower. Faced with local stone of a silver-grey and golden hue, the palace looks as if it is perpetually wreathed in a light mist, which further enhances the romantic air of this unique edifice.
After Orlov's death, Catherine bought Gatchina and subsequently gave it to her son Paul in 1783. "Gatchina Palace and Paul! The two are inseparable, they are so well suited and have exercised such a strong influence on one another. The strange, enigmatic Emperor, and the strange 'incomprehensible' palace. Yet most surprising of all is the fact that the palace was not intended for Paul, although it seems to have been made for him. It is hard to imagine anything other than the royal Gatchina recluse when we recall the life of Catherine the Great's heir. Paul left such a mark on the 'spirit' of the Gatchina buildings that it seems only fair to call Gatchina Paul's creation" (Nikolai Lanceray).
Vincenzo Brenna, Paul's favourite architect, altered the external appearance of the palace somewhat, increasing the height of the outbuildings on either side. The right-hand wing, once occupied by the stables, was converted into a storeroom, which came to house a collection of weapons and was thus referred to as the Arsenal.
In front of the palace, the existing meadow was transformed into a huge square, bordered by a moat and a stone wall. Drawbridges spanned the former, while cannons could be seen protruding from the embrasures in the wall. These were fired on public holidays and to mark the arrival of distinguished guests.
Like a true castle, the palace had its own underground passageway, which stretched northwards from the building for a distance

**420**
Gatchina Palace. Marble Dining Room

**421**
Gatchina Palace. Anteroom

**422**
Gatchina Palace. Paul I's Throne Room

of 120 metres. It was installed in Orlov's day, and Brenna later rebuilt and reinforced the tunnel walls.

Under Paul I, the palace apartments too underwent significant changes. Not only were they adapted to meet the needs of their imperial residents, but they were also decorated in fine style. The Marble Dining Room, for example, gained a new ceremonial air as a result of the magnificent fittings, central to which was the fireplace, embellished with a beautifully framed mirror. The once modest study of the master of the house became Paul I's grandiose Throne Room and, in turn, the architectural centrepiece of the palace ensemble. On the second floor, notable for its simple décor, the Emperor's sons had their suites.

After 1796, Gatchina was raised to the status of a town by order of the Emperor. A town hall, hospital, college, church and post office

were built there, along with glassworks and a porcelain factory.
After the death of Paul I, Gatchina passed to his widow, Maria Fedorovna, and from her to Nicholas I in 1828. Like Paul before them, the last emperors also paid frequent visits to this picturesque suburb of Petersburg.
In the 1840s, the architect Roman Kuzmin transformed the modest Arsenal into a new palace. Over two hundred state and private rooms were fitted out on the first floor for the use of the families of Nicholas I and later Alexander II and Alexander III. On the ground floor, around the edges of the building, were chambers for the court attendants. A statue of Paul I, designed by Ivan Vitali, was installed in the centre of the square.
During the time that it was inhabited by the ruling elite, Gatchina Palace became renowned for its splendid, imposing and beautiful interiors, the décor of which reflected the changing styles of the times. It also became the home of a splendid collection of Russian and Western European paintings and objects of applied art, all of which revealed the personal tastes and predilections of the palace's owners. Alexander III was particularly fond of Gatchina and chose it as his permanent abode, prompting his contemporaries to nickname him "the hermit of Gatchina."
The Gatchina residence is interesting not only as a splendid park and palace ensemble, but also as a witness to numerous important historical events and the political and personal secrets of the imperial family.
At present fundamental restoration work is in progress, and the vast park surrounding the palace is emerging once more as one of the most beautiful natural settings in Russia.

**423, 424**
Gatchina Palace. White Room
Late 18th century, architects: Antonio Rinaldi, Vincenzo Brenna

**425**
Gatchina Palace. Maria Fedorovna's Throne Room
Late 18th century, architect: Vincenzo Brenna

**426**
Gatchina Palace. State Bedroom
Ceiling painting *The Wedding of Psyche.*
1799, artist: Gabriel François Doyen

## Gatchina Park

The magnificent Gatchina Park complex comprises three parks, the most significant of which is the Palace Park. The latter covers an area of 143 hectares, almost a third of which is occupied by lakes that are dotted with islands, which in turn are linked by bridges of various styles. One of the most striking of these is the Humpback Bridge, which has become a unique symbol of Gatchina. It is quite rightly considered to be one of the most beautiful monuments to Russian Classicism. The bridge also serves as an excellent vantage point from which the wonderful surroundings can be viewed: "nowhere else but here can you get a real feel for the unique beauty of Gatchina with its abundance of water and woods. The towers of the palace are just visible from here, like the towers of Sleeping Beauty's castle" (Vladimir Makarov).

Beside the walls of the palace itself, on an artificially created plot of land, lies the Private Garden, one of four small, regular gardens in the western part of the Palace Park. From here, a flight of granite steps led up to Paul's personal apartments. Decorated with marble sculptures acquired by the Emperor during his travels around Italy, the garden resembled a unique open-air stateroom. Only Paul himself and his personal guests had the right to admire the scenery, hence its name.

A similar regular garden, created for the quiet leisure of select society, was laid out on the Island of Love near the northern shore of the White Lake, the largest in the park. The island's main feature is the Temple of Venus, which was an almost exact replica of the one in the grounds of Prince de Conde's estate in Chantilly. The Venus Pavilion is visible from all angles yet blends organically with its surroundings, making it a delightful ornament to this part of the park.

The small Priory Park lies in a separate part of the grounds on the shore of the Black Lake. This quiet wooded area became the setting for the Priory, a symbol of "romantic" Gatchina. While in France, Paul, the Grand Master of the Knights of Malta, visited the priory dedicated to the order and belonging to Prince de Conde. On his return to Russia, he decided to build a similar house for himself on his country estate.

**427**
Private Garden. 1794–1797, architect: Vincenzo Brenna

**428**
Gatchina Park. Humpback bridge on Long Island
1800–1801, architect: Andrean Zakharov

**429**
Gatchina Park. Temple of Venus on the Island of Love. 1792–1793

**430**
Priory on the shore of the Black Lake
1797–1799, architect: Nikolai Lvov

## The Landscapes of Gatchina

Set far away from the sea, Gatchina has a feature that is rare to the other imperial estates outside Petersburg, namely, vast stretches of water. An area of 36 hectares or approximately a quarter of the entire grounds is occupied by lakes.
Enchanting views of still waters framed by the greenery of parks and meadows are what make the landscapes of Gatchina unique.
The lakes with their countless islands and channels fed by the waters of the Gatchinka and Kolpanka Rivers create an intricately interwoven system of waterways against the background of which the palace, pavilions, bridges,

gates, terraces and viewing grounds look so utterly picturesque, adding a musical quality to the atmosphere reigning the park, which has been described as the "symphony of the North".
The largest body of water is the White Lake with an area of 20 hectares and a depth of 12 metres. It was evidently given its name because of the incredible purity and transparency of the water. From the White Lake flows the Izhora River, while nearby lie the Zakharov, Marshy, Swan and Crow Islands, the Island of Love and a number of small, artificial islets, including the Fir, Pine and Birch Islets named after the types of trees planted on them.
The islands, including the so-called Long Island that stretches from north to south, enliven the still expanses of the lakes with their plant life and manmade features such as the Venus Pavilion on the Island of Love, the Humpback Bridge and the Jetty on Long Island, the Admiralty and the Water Labyrinth.
One of Gatchina's most beautiful lakes is the Silver Lake, famed for its crystal clear water with a silvery luminescence. The lake is fed by underground springs that bubble away below the surface, creating the illusion of a silvery glow. Notably, this lake does not freeze over in winter. It is also known as the "Emerald Lake": a layer of coloured clay on the bottom of the lake lends the clear water a green hue.

**431**
Panorama of Gatchina Park

**432**
Palace Park. Metal Bridge over the Water Labyrinth. 1880s, architect: L.F. Sperer

**433**
Vladimir Makovsky. 1846–1920
*Portrait of Empress Maria Fedorovna.* 1912

# Oranienbaum

The park and palace ensemble at Oranienbaum lies to the southwest of Petersburg. Its origins are linked to the name of Peter I's friend and associate, Alexander Menshikov, who was given the land in 1710 by the Emperor himself. Having been presented with a vast expanse of land on the southern shore of the Gulf of Finland, Menshikov, the first governor of St Petersburg decided to build a residence close to the imperial estate at Peterhof and the island of Kotlin on which the Kronstadt Fortress was being built. After Peter's death, Menshikov assumed the leading role in the government of Russia. The very best architects, sculptors and carvers in the land were enlisted to work on his palace. The overall design of the Great Palace, often referred to as the Menshikov Palace, was the work of Andreas Schlüter. The central two-storey section is linked by ground floor galleries to two side wings, referred to as the Church Wing and the Japanese Wing. Above the tall double-ledged roof typical of the Petrine era soars a tower, a belvedere adorned with a crown. The palace was erected on a high terrace overlooking the gulf and the outlying parks. It is in the building's indissoluble link with the surrounding landscape that its true charm lies.

**434**
Great (Menshikov) Palace. 1711–1727, architects: Giovanni Mario Fontana, Johann Braunstein, Gottfried Schaedel

**435**
Upper Park in the vicinity of the Chinese Palace
The Three Graces. Early 19th century. France, unknown sculptor
(copy of a marble group by G. Pilon)

**436**
Upper Park. Flowerbed in front of the north façade of the Chinese Palace

## Peterstadt

In 1743, Elizabeth Petrovna bestowed Oranienbaum upon her nephew and Peter the Great's grandson, the future Emperor Peter III. This "strange" figure cast a mysterious shadow over the history of Russia, and his absurd life and tragic death still arouse great interest today. He came to the throne as a result of one of Elizabeth's whims, but his coarse tastes, unwholesome habits and contempt for all things Russian and Orthodox led to his inevitable demise. Within just one year, Peter III had succeeded in turning the whole of Russian society against him. His subjects could not forgive his admiration for King Frederick II of Prussia and his betrayal of the interests of the Russian nation. Peter III's wife, Catherine, a clever and highly educated woman succeeded in exploiting these circumstances, playing on the loyal sentiments of the officers of the guards. The Orlov brothers, who lead a coup against Peter III, forced him to sign a letter of abdication on 28 June 1762. This historic event took place within the walls of the Great Palace at Oranienbaum, after which the Emperor was taken to Ropsha, where he was killed on 7 July 1762.

In the Upper Park at Oranienbaum a palace and park ensemble comprising Peter's Palace, the Honorary Gates and the Peter Park was created in honour of the crown prince, the future Emperor Peter III, and named Peterstadt. At the same time, a palace was built which remains standing to this day. This was Antonio Rinaldi's first project in Russia. It is a simple and modest structure with the appearance of a cosy two-storey house with small rooms. A spiral staircase leads to the first floor where Peter's chambers were located. The largest and most beautiful room in the palace is the Picture Hall where the rows of canvases have a particularly striking effect. The panels, doors and wooden surrounds are covered with varnished imitation Chinese designs in accordance with the style of the times. The walls of the remaining rooms are upholstered with coloured fabrics.

**437**
Peterstadt. Peter III's Palace
1758–1762, architect: Antonio Rinaldi

**438**
Peter III's Palace in Peterstadt. Picture Hall

**439**
Lucas Conrad Pfandzelt. *Portrait of Peter III*

**440**
Peterstadt. Honorary Gates. 1757, architect: Antonio Rinaldi

**The Sliding Hill Pavilion**

The Private Villa ensemble was built on lands purchased in the early 1760s by the princess of Anhalt-Zerbst who was given the Orthodox name of Ekaterina Alexeevna and went on to become Catherine the Great. Only a few of the many buildings designed by Rinaldi and erected in this part of the Upper Park remain. Of these, "Her Highness the Empress's little house," later known as the Chinese Palace, and the Sliding Hill Pavilion are worthy of special note. The design of the surrounding park is based upon a combination of the principles of landscape and regular gardening. The Sliding Hill Pavilion is the only remaining architectural component of an enormous complex structure made up of open galleries and multiple slopes.

The elegant, three-storey, 33 metre high pavilion, situated at the top of a tall incline, is a dominant feature of the Upper Park. The building is essentially circular with three rectangles placed symmetrically around it. The idea behind it sprung from the traditional Russian winter leisure pursuit of sledging down icy slopes. Sliding Hills, ridden on a sledge in winter or in a special wheeled cart in summer, served as yet another of the diversions of 18th-century court society. The Sliding Hill at Oranienbaum was modelled on one built at Tsarskoye Selo by Bartolomeo Rastrelli to designs by K. Nartov

and a similar structure in the court village of Pokrovskoye near Moscow.
The main room of the Sliding Hill Pavilion, known as the Round Hall takes the form of a rotunda crowned with a dome. Three square appurtenances are arranged around it. The first floor is girded by a colonnaded gallery, while an open terrace is situated on the second floor. This system of tiers gives the building a unique appearance.
The Round Hall is the largest room in the Pavilion and is decorated with ornamental stuccowork and murals. The unusual floor is paved with artificial marble bearing an intricate painted design. Meanwhile, the Porcelain Study is decorated in the whimsical and elegant style of the Rococo. The plaster figures of monkeys, cupids and birds that support the shelves filled with Meissen porcelain are particularly worthy of note.

**441**
Sliding Hill Pavilion
1762–1774, architect: Antonio Rinaldi

**442**
Sliding Hill Pavilion. Round Hall. Late 1760s – early 1770s, architect: Antonio Rinaldi, artist: Serafino Barozzi

**443**
Sliding Hill Pavilion. Porcelain Study. Late 1760s – early 1770s, architect: Antonio Rinaldi

**444**
Sliding Hill Pavilion. Porcelain Study
The Triumph of Venus. 1772–1774
Meissen. Porcelain

## The Chinese Palace

Amongst the surviving buildings of the Private Villa ensemble, the most remarkable is the edifice that later came to be known as the Chinese Palace: "a veritable wonder of 18th-century wonders." Humble on the outside, it is distinguished by the unmatched perfection and exquisite splendour of its interiors.
In the 18th-century, *chinoiserie*, based upon Chinese motifs, became widespread in Russian decorative art. The Chinese Palace is an outstanding example of this style. Moreover, it houses an exquisite collection of genuine Chinese works of art. The centrepiece of the palace interior is the large stateroom, which opens out onto further suites of rooms to the east and west. To the west, the state suites terminate in the Large Chinese Study (the Billiard Room) which boasts a highly original design. As in so many of Rinaldi's creations at Oranienbaum, the corners of the room are rounded and the walls and ceiling meet in a smooth curve. The furnishings reflect the fantastical notion of China that was held by the people who designed and decorated them. The walls are decorated with wooden panels depicting scenes of Chinese life set against the background of a landscape.

**445**
Chinese Palace. 1762–1768, architect: Antonio Rinaldi
**446**
Chinese Palace. Muse Room
**447**
Flowerbed in front of the north façade of the Chinese Palace
Omphale. Early 18th century. Russia, unknown sculptor
**448**
Chinese Palace. Muse Room. Detail of a mural

The entire composition is complemented by the illustration of *The Union of Europe and Asia* on the ceiling (mid-19th century, artists: Serafino and Giuseppe Barozzi).

To the east of the Great Hall lies the Bugle-work Room, which was a wonder of applied art in its heyday. The room was decorated with twelve bugled panels set in gilded carved frames and depicting fantastic scenes of tropical forests teeming with birds and dotted with ornamental bridges and gazebos picked out in silks.

The opulence and originality of the room's fittings are further enhanced by the moulded plaster panel over the fireplace – one of the finest examples of stuccowork in the palace – and the ornamental parquet floor. Approximately 750 square metres of floor space are covered with decorative parquet flooring. Antonio Rinaldi developed such original designs and used such a wide variety of woods that the floors of the Chinese Palace are believed to be absolutely unique.

The Lilac Drawing Room, named after the colour of its walls, was designed for relaxation. The walls are decorated for the most part with elegant stuccowork in the Rococo style, depicting vases of flowers, garlands, creeping vines, leaves and shells. Hence, the room also became known as the *Plastered Retreat*. Garlands wind their way exquisitely across the pinkish purple walls and climb up towards the ceiling.

**449**
Chinese Palace. Buglework Room

**450**
Chinese Palace. Chinese vase. 16th century
Porcelain

**451**
Chinese Palace. Boudoir. 1760s, architect: Antonio Rinaldi, artists: Serafino Barozzi and Stefano Torelli

**452**
Chinese Palace. Great Hall

**453**
Chinese Palace. Large Chinese Study (Billiard Room)

## The Parks of Oranienbaum

To the north of the Great Palace is the Lower Garden, one of the first regular parks in Russia, decorated with sculptures, fountains, elegant flowerbeds and hedges. The vast Upper Park lies to the south of the Great Palace. It was developed at a time when park designers were already beginning to turn away from the "regular" style and emphasise the natural beauty of the landscape instead. The park and palace ensembles of Oranienbaum are the unique creations of Rinaldi. The architect devoted almost twenty of his thirty years in Russia to them. Yet it is not only the carefully conceived design of the Upper Park ensembles, the originality of the architectural styles of the buildings and the artistic value of their interior décor that make it possible to speak of the exceptional nature of Oranienbaum. More importantly, the land was not captured by the Germans during the war, although the enemy besieged the town for 29 months. Nor was the park and palace complex reduced to ruins. The monuments of Oranienbaum are not replicas of artworks of a bygone era, but are original in every sense of the word.

**454**
Chinese Palace. Muse Room. Detail of the interior
**455, 458**
Sliding Hill Pavilion. 1762–1764, architect: Antonio Rinaldi
**456**
Chinese Palace. North façade
**457**
Upper Park. Statue: *Diana the Huntress.* 18th century

# Kronstadt

Twenty nine kilometres from the mouth of the Neva, on the island of Kotlin in the Gulf of Finland, the fortress of Kronschlot was consecrated in the presence of Peter the Great on 7 May 1704. The Emperor himself chose the site of this stronghold and at one time even considered founding the capital there. Responsibility for overseeing the construction of the sea fort, which was to defend the waters of the Neva, was conferred upon Alexander Menshikov. Kronschlot saw its first military action in June 1704, and over the course of the next two centuries the sailors stationed there fulfilled the Emperor's instructions to the letter: "To defend this citadel... to the last man, whatever happens."

Besides the installation of the fortress, batteries and fortified harbours, work was started on the creation of a system of canals and the construction of docks, some of which are still in use today.

Under the protection of the fortress, a town began to take shape in 1714 with straight streets and canals designed to drain the marshy, low-lying land. Like Petersburg, the town was developed according to a specific plan. In contrast to the nearby metropolis, however, this small town, christened Kronstadt in 1723, has borne the same name to this day.

From the very beginning, Kronstadt was envisaged not only as a habitation for sailors and soldiers, but also as a major port, which was supposed to play an important part in local trade.

**459**
Warships in Petrovskaya harbour

**460**
On duty

**461**
Anchor Square. Naval Cathedral. 1903–1913, architect: Vasily Kosiakov, artist and architect: N. Podberezsky
Monument to Admiral Stepan Makarov. 1913, sculptor: Leonid Sherwood

Kronstadt is a city of maritime glory, and all of its most interesting edifices and monuments reflect this theme. Amongst the religious architecture, the most significant building is undoubtedly the Naval Cathedral on Anchor Square, the historic centre of the city. The square was named in 1754 when a warehouse for storing anchors and chains taken from defunct vessels was erected upon it. The cathedral at Kronstadt was intended to serve as a memorial to "members of the Naval Department who died in the performance of their duties."
The cathedral is an impressive example of the late Byzantine style. The Naval Cathedral is essentially a square, elongated to the east and west by two semicircles. It stands at a height of 70.62 metres, and the large cupola is 26.7 metres in diameter.

**462**
The embankment of Obvodny Canal

**463**
Anchors and chains around the monument to Stepan Makarov

**464**
Monument to Emperor Peter I
1841, sculptor: T. Jaques, cast by Piotr Klodt

Петру Перьвому
Основателю
Кронштадта
841 Года